中华传统美德

TRADITIONAL VIRTUES OF CHINA

“符号中国”编写组◎编著

中央民族大学出版社
China Minzu University Press

图书在版编目(CIP)数据

中华传统美德 ：汉文、英文 / “符号中国”编写组编著. — 北京：中央民族大学出版社, 2024.9

（符号中国）

ISBN 978-7-5660-2285-1

Ⅰ. ①中…　Ⅱ. ①符…　Ⅲ. ①品德教育—介绍—中国—汉、英　Ⅳ. ①D648

中国国家版本馆CIP数据核字（2024）第016652号

符号中国：中华传统美德 TRADITIONAL VIRTUES OF CHINA

编　　著　“符号中国”编写组
策划编辑　沙　平
责任编辑　李苏幸
英文编辑　邱　械
美术编辑　曹　娜　郑亚超　洪　涛
出版发行　中央民族大学出版社
　　　　　北京市海淀区中关村南大街27号　　邮编：100081
　　　　　电话：（010）68472815（发行部）　传真：（010）68933757（发行部）
　　　　　　　　（010）68932218（总编室）　　　　（010）68932447（办公室）
经 销 者　全国各地新华书店
印 刷 厂　北京兴星伟业印刷有限公司
开　　本　787 mm×1092 mm　1/16　印张：8.5
字　　数　118千字
版　　次　2024年9月第1版　2024年9月第1次印刷
书　　号　ISBN 978-7-5660-2285-1
定　　价　58.00元

本册编写者

刘　涛

中国素有“礼仪之邦”的美誉。重视个人的道德修养，重视社会的道德教化，这种传统美德是中华民族精神的重要特征和组成部分。

中华民族传统美德的形成和发展已

China is known as "a state of ceremonies". With the importance of personal moral cultivation and mass moral education, the traditional virtue is an important component and trait of Chinese national spirit.

The formation and development of the

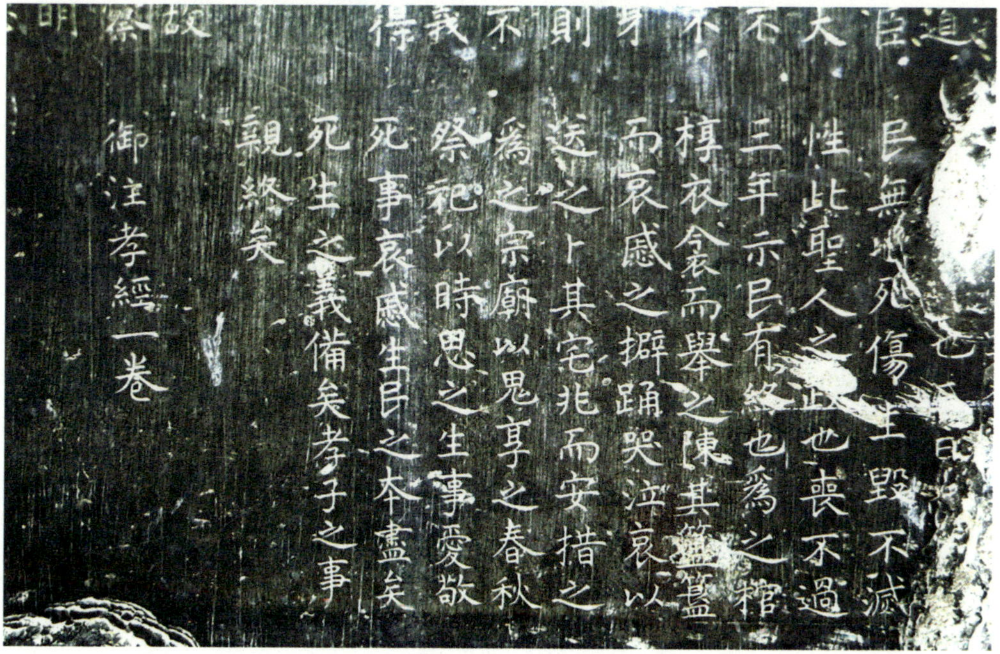

经有几千年的历史，从口头传承到文字记载，内容博大精深，并且在不断地发展完善。这种美德是中国人处理人与人之间的关系、处理人与社会的关系和人与自然的关系的实践结晶，自然地体现在每个中国人的言行之中。本书通过中国人的嘉言和懿行来讨论传承数千年的传统美德，选取了许多古人的故事，以此展现中华传统美德。

traditional virtues of the Chinese nation has a history of thousands of years, from oral tradition to written records. Given the continuous development and improvement, its content is broad and profound. The virtue is the summarization and sublimation of the way of interaction between people, between man and society, between man and nature, which is reflected in everyday life naturally. This book discusses the traditional virtues of the Chinese tradition of thousands of years through edifying words and exemplary conduct, and selects many tales of the ancients, to show the Chinese traditional virtue.

目 录 Contents

中华传统美德概述

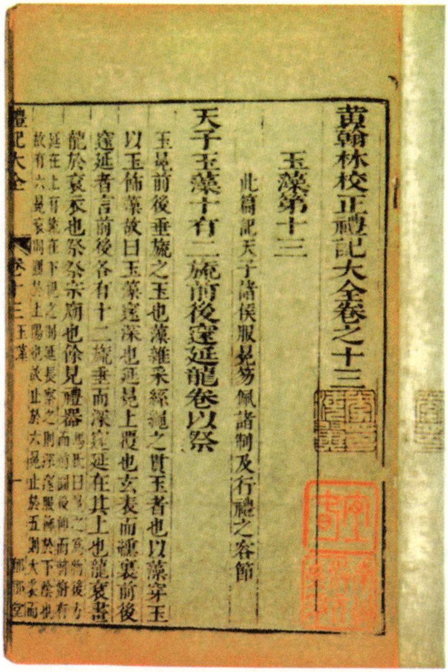
黄翰林校正禮記大全卷之十三
玉藻第十三
此篇記天子諸侯服冕笏佩諸制及行禮之容節
天子玉藻十有二旒前後邃延龍卷以祭
玉冕前後垂旒之玉也藻雜采絲繩之貫玉者也以藻穿玉
以玉飾藻故曰玉藻邃深也延冕上覆也玄表而纁裏前後
邃延者言前後各有十二旒垂而深邃延在其上也龍卷畫
龍於衮衣也祭祭宗廟也餘見禮器
禮記大全 卷十三 玉藻

个人美德

家庭美德

中华传统美德概述

The Summary of the Traditional Chinese Virtues

美德即美好的品德，是指那些积极的、向上的、崇高的、引导人与社会向善的品德。而品德则是对人的言行的规范，有的通过书面的法律、法令、著作等方式流传下来，有的通过一代又一代人的言传身教传承下来。法律通过国家的力量对人进行制约，品德则是通过个人的力量从内对人进行制约。

中华传统美德是中华民族五千年继承下来的优秀道德遗产，内容可谓博大精深，涉及社会生活的方方面面。其核心思想是仁、义、礼、智、信，在此基础上又包括修身、齐家、治国、平天下这四个层面。

Virtue equals morals, referring to the positive, upward and exalted characters guiding people and the society to goodness. The moral is the guidance of people's words and deeds, some handed down by ways of written laws, decrees, works, etc., and some passed down through precepts and lessons from generation to generation. Laws restrict people through the national power, and moral restricts people through inner personal power.

Chinese traditional virtues are the excellent ethics heritage of the Chinese nation through five thousand years, whose contents are broad and profound, involving all aspects of social life. Their core thought are benevolence, righteousness, propriety, wisdom and faith, on this basis, extending to four aspects of self-cultivation and regulating the family, country and world.

> 传统美德的核心思想

仁、义、礼、智、信是中华传统美德的核心观念，也是儒家思想的核心，称为“五常”。这“五常”始终贯穿于中华民族的伦理发展，是古代中国价值体系中最核心的因素。

仁，即人与人之间相处的规范和准则，人们要相亲相爱，互相帮助。中国一直重视伦理关系，尤其强调人与人之间的和谐相处。因此，仁在中国有着极为重要的地位，是五常的核心，是一切美德之源。中国伟大的思想家孔子（前551—前479年）将“仁”定义为“爱人”，并解释说：“夫仁者，己欲立而立人，己欲达而达人。”意思是：仁德的人，自己若想成功，那么首先要使别人成功；自己

> The Core Ideas of the Traditional Virtues

Benevolence, righteousness, propriety, wisdom and faith are the core concept of Chinese traditional virtues, and also the core thought of Confucian thoughts, known as *Wuchang* (cardinal virtues). This *Wuchang* runs through the ethical development of the Chinese nation, which was the first core factor in the value system of ancient China.

Ren (benevolence) is namely the norm and standard of interaction between human beings. People need to be kind with and help each other. China has always attached importance to ethics and morals, with particular emphasis on the harmonious coexistence between human beings. Therefore, benevolence in China has the extremely important status, which is the core of *Wuchang* and the source of all virtues. The great Chinese thinker Confucius (551 B.C.- 479 B.C.)

颐和园仁寿殿

中国古代许多建筑都以“仁”字命名，如颐和园的仁寿殿。

Renshou Temple of the Summer Palace

Many ancient Chinese buildings are named *Ren*, such as the *Renshou* Temple of the Summer Palace.

若想被人理解，那么首先要理解他人。孔子还说：“能行五者于天下，为仁矣。”意思是能做到恭敬、宽容、守信、才智敏捷、怀有恩惠之心这五方面，那么就能称其为“仁”了。“仁”的品德体现在中国社会的方方面面，如人际交往上讲究仁爱、仁至义尽，政治上讲究仁政、仁治。现在中国的睦邻友好、和平共处等外交政策也可以从这里找到哲学依据。

defined benevolence as giving love, and elaborated: he who themselves are to be successful should first make other people successful; he who themselves are to be understood should first understand others. Confucius also said if you can be respectful, tolerant, honest, intelligent and having the heart of grace, all these five aspects and then you could be called benevolence. Benevolence reflected in all aspects of life, such as kindheartedness, being gracious and dutiful, political stressing on the policy of benevolence and lenient governing. Now China's peaceful coexistence with neighboring countries could also trace its philosophical basis from here.

Yi (righteousness) means fair and reasonable. Confucius said a gentleman should be impartial and fair. China attaches great importance to the virtue of righteousness. The Chinese ancient great thinker Mencius (approx. 372 B.C.-289

• 杭州岳王庙里的“忠义常昭”匾额
Horizontal Inscribed Board of "Often Showing Loyalty" in Temple of Yue Fei, Hangzhou

义，指公正、合理。孔子曰：“君子寓于义”，意思是君子处事应当公正、公平，中国非常重视义这一美德。中国古代伟大的思想家孟子（约前372—前289年）曰：“生亦我所欲也，义亦我所欲也，二者不可得兼，舍生而取义者也。”意思是，生命是我想要的，正义也是我想要的，如果二者不能同时得到，那么宁可选择正义而舍去生命。义反映在中国日常生活的方方面面，如在国家的层面，要讲求正义，公平合理地处理各种关系；朋友交往要讲求义气，互相帮助；而夫妻之间则要重情义，用心经营自己的婚姻。

礼，指礼仪、礼节，是国家与国家之间、人与人之间交往和相处

B.C.) said life was what I wanted, and I wanted justice, too; if I could not get both at the same time, I would rather choose justice and give life. Righteousness reflects in daily life, such as at the national level, emphasizing the justice, dealing with various relations fairly and reasonably; being loyal to friends and help each other; between husband and wife, treasuring and cherishing their marriage.

Li (propriety) indicates etiquette and formality, which is ancient laws and regulations and code of conduct between nations, and the interpersonal communication. Propriety is an important part of ancient Chinese law. Chinese have attached importance to propriety since ancient times, thinking only politeness can maintain the long-term stability of the

的典章制度和行为规范。礼是中国古代法律的重要组成部分。中国人自古便重视礼，认为讲礼才可以维持社会的长治久安，因此中国素有“礼仪之邦”之称。孔子说：“不学礼，无以立。”意思是如果不学习礼，不践行礼，那么就不能在人世间立足。在中国古代，礼存在于

community, so China is known as a state of ceremonies. Confucius said if you did not learn the ceremony and practice the ceremony, you could not gain a foothold in this world. In ancient China, propriety existed in all kinds of social relations, and was peremptory, e.g. to define hierarchy between the monarch and his subjects, mainly as subjects in awe of the monarch;

天子九鼎

Emperor's Nine Cauldrons

诸侯七鼎

Seigneurs' Seven Cauldrons

卿大夫五鼎

Officers' Five Cauldrons

士三鼎

Bachelors' Three Cauldrons

- **周代礼器制度**

礼器产生于原始社会晚期，是中国古代的贵族在举行祭祀、征战、宴请等礼仪活动时使用的器物，用以表明使用者的身份、等级和权力。

Sacrificial Vessel System of the Zhou Dynasty

Sacrificial vessels originated in the late primitive society, which are containers used by the ancient Chinese nobility when holding ceremonial activities as sacrifices, conquests, feasts, etc., in ordor to show the user's identity, class and power.

各种社会关系之中，且具有强制力，如君臣之间要守礼，主要表现为臣民对君主的敬畏；师生之间要守礼，主要表现为学生要尊敬老师，而老师也不能妄自尊大。

智，是指智慧、知识与经验，意味着知对错、明善恶，要具有较高的见识，对一件事的性质有正确的理解和判断，对于事情的未来发展有预测。孔子说：“智者不

to regulate conducts between the teachers and students, mainly for the students to respect teachers, and the teachers to be not arrogant.

Zhi (wisdom) referring to knowledge and experience, means to know right from wrong and good from evil. One should have wider experiences, correct understanding and judgment of the nature of things, and have the prediction for its future development. Confucius said that as long as there was wisdom, we would

• 孔子像
Portrait of Confucius

惑。”就是指只要有智慧，面对问题就不会迷惑，在关键时刻就能够做出正确的决断，从而解决问题。中国一直非常重视智这一美德，智体现在生活的各个方面。无论是政治决策、社会管理，还是家庭生活、个人为人处世，都需要智慧。

信，指诚信、信义、信用，是治国和人际交往的基本原则之一。中国人一直崇尚诚信，古人云：“对人以诚信，人不欺我；对事以诚信，事无不成。”意思是对待别人要用一颗真诚的心，别人便会尊敬自己；做任何事情都用诚信去对待，才会获得成功。

not be confused when facing problem. We could make the right decision at the critical moment, thereby solving the problem. China has always attached great importance to the virtue of wisdom. Wisdom is reflected in all aspects of life, whether political decision, social management, or family life and personal interaction with others.

Xin (faith) refers to trustworthiness, integrity and credibility, which is one of the basic principles in nation governance and interpersonal relationships. Chinese have always been advocating honesty. The ancients said that to treat people with a sincere heart, others would respect you; to do everything with integrity, you could be successful.

儒家

儒家思想是中国古代具有影响力的思想学派，是中国人的基本文化信仰。儒家思想由春秋时期的伟大思想家孔子创立，后经西汉思想家董仲舒发展成为中国封建社会占主要统治地位的学派。儒家思想以“仁”为核心，崇尚“仁、义、礼、智、信”，提倡“忠恕”（以对待自己的态度对待他人）和“中庸”（中正平和）之道，主张“德治”（以道德感化教育人）、“仁政”（宽厚仁慈的统治），重视伦理道德。

Confucian

Confucianism is an influential school of thought in ancient China, which is a basic cultural beliefs of the Chinese people. Confucianism was founded by the great thinker Confucius in the Spring and Autumn Period, and then developed into a dominant school of thought in China by the thinker Dong Zhongshu in the Western Han Dynasty. Confucianism takes benevolence as the core, advocates benevolence, righteousness, propriety, wisdom and faith, as well as *Zhongshu* (to treat others in the way of treating oneself) and *Zhongyong* (peaceful and impartial), proposes rule of virtue (to teach people with moral education) and policy of benevolence (benevolent rule), paying attention to ethics.

- 《孔子圣迹图》（清 焦秉贞）
  Picture of Confucius, by Jiao Bingzhen (Qing Dynasty)

> 传统美德的根基

几乎每一个中国人自幼就知道“修身、齐家、治国、平天下”这句真言。此言出自西汉典章制

> The Foundation of the Traditional Virtues

Almost every Chinese knows the proverb of self-cultivation and regulating the family, henceforth ruling the country and dominating the world from their childhood. It came from *The Book of Rites*, Western Han-dynasty's laws and institutions books. It says those who want to work in just ways and carry forward the ancient virtues of the people in the world, have first to govern their country

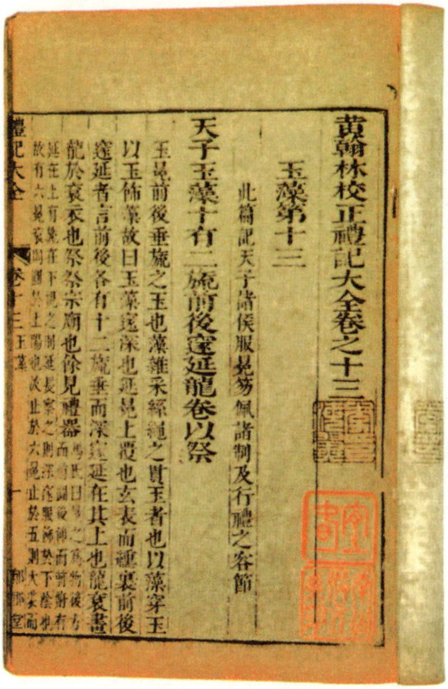
黄翰林校正禮記大全卷之十三
玉藻第十三
此篇記天子諸侯服冕笏佩諸制及行禮之容節
天子玉藻十有二旒前後邃延龍卷以祭
玉冕前後垂旒之玉也藻雜采絲繩之貫玉者也以藻穿玉
以玉飾藻故曰玉藻邃深也延冕上覆也玄表而纁裏前後
邃延者言前後各有十二旒垂而深邃延在其上也龍衮畫
龍於衮衣也祭祭宗廟也餘見禮器

• 《礼记》书影

《礼记》阐述了哲学、社会生活、政治、伦理、宗教等各个方面的思想，其中《大学》《中庸》《礼运》等篇目对后世的影响非常深远。

Photocopy of *The Book of Rites*

The Book of Rites describes the thought of various aspects, such as philosophy, social life, politics, ethics, religion, etc., among which *The Great Learning*, *The Doctrine of Mean*, *Evolutions of Rites*, etc., have a very far-reaching impact on future generations.

度书籍《礼记》："古之欲明明德于天下者，先治其国；欲治其国者，先齐其家；欲齐其家者，先修其身……身修而后家齐，家齐而后国治，国治而后天下平。"意思是：古代那些要想在天下弘扬光明正大品德的人，先要治理好自己的国家；要想治理好自己的国家，先要管理好自己的家庭和家族；要想管理好自己

well; to govern their country well, he who have first to manage his own home and family well; to manage their own home and family well, he who have first to cultivate one's moral character...after the cultivation of one's moral character, one can manage a household well; after a good family management, one can govern the country well; after a good government of the country, the world would become pacific.

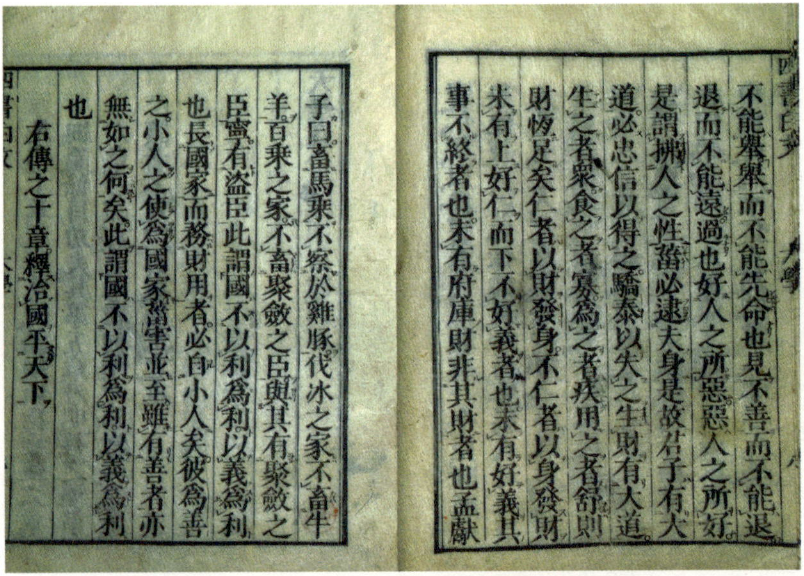
四書白文 大學
不能舉舉而不能先命也見不善而不能退
退而不能遠過也好人之所惡惡人之所好
是謂拂人之性菑必逮夫身是故君子有大
道必忠信以得之驕泰以失之生財有大道
生之者衆食之者寡爲之者疾用之者舒則
財恆足矣仁者以財發身不仁者以身發財
未有上好仁而下不好義者也未有好義其
事不終者也未有府庫財非其財者也孟獻
子曰畜馬乘不察於雞豚伐冰之家不畜牛
羊百乘之家不畜聚斂之臣與其有聚斂之
臣寧有盜臣此謂國不以利爲利以義爲利
也長國家而務財用者必自小人矣彼爲善
之小人之使爲國家菑害並至雖有善者亦
無如之何矣此謂國不以利爲利以義爲利
也
右傳之十章釋治國平天下
四書白文

• 明代《四书白文》中"治国平天下"的言论（图片提供：微图）
The Word on "Politics of Regulating the Country and World" in *The Four Books of Baiwen* in the Ming Dynasty

的家庭和家族，先要修养自身的品性……品性修养后，才能管理好家庭和家族；家庭和家族管理好了，才能治理好国家；治理好国家，天下才能太平。

“修身、齐家、治国、平天下”，相辅相成，缺一不可，构成了中国人传统道德理想的根基。以此为基础，中华传统美德不断完善发展，大致可以分为四个层面。一是个人修养的层面：这是中华传统美德的基础，包括勤奋、勇敢、谦虚、节俭、慎独、智慧、恒心、诚实、守信这九种美德。二是家庭的层面：家庭在中国具有重要的地位，是沟通个人和社会的枢纽，因此处理好家庭关系极其重要。家庭关系大致包括父子、夫妇、兄弟等几种关系。三是社会的层面：社会有诸多关系，包括个人和国家的关系、师生关系、朋友关系、邻里关系以及陌生人与陌生人的关系等。四是自然的层面：中国人一直强调天、地、人和谐相处，因此人类应该遵守人的本分，不能以自然的主人自居而肆意妄为。

Self-cultivation and regulating the family, country and world complement each other, and are indispensable, which constitute the foundation of the Chinese traditional moral ideal. On this basis, the Chinese traditional virtue continuously improves and develops. It can be divided into four levels. The first is the level of personal accomplishment which is the basis of Chinese traditional virtue, including nine characteristics: diligent, brave, humble, thrifty, self-restraining, wise, perseverant, honest and trustworthy. The second is the level of family. Family has an important position in China, which is the ribbon between individuals and society, so it's very important to deal with family relationship. Family relations include parents and children, husband and wife, brothers and sisters. The third is the level of society. Society is comprised of a lot of social relations including citizen-country relationship, teacher-student relationship, friendship, neighbor relationship and the relationship between strangers. The fourth is the level of nature. Chinese has always stressed the harmony among heaven, the earth and human being, so human being should abide by one's duty, and cannot consider

• 山西平遥古城的“正心修身”匾额
Plaque of "Upright Heart and Self-cultivation" in the Ancient City of Pingyao, Shanxi

谈论中华传统美德就要从个人、家庭、社会和自然这四个方面着手，如此才可以全面地了解中华传统美德。

oneself to be the master of nature and do what one wishes without restraint.

Talking on Chinese traditional virtues will begin from these four aspects as the individual, family, society and nature, so you can fully understand the Chinese traditional virtues.

个人美德

Personal Virtues

个人品德是指个人通过自觉的道德修养和社会道德教育，所形成的稳定的心理状态和行为习惯，这是其他品德的基础。中华传统美德中的个人美德有诸多方面，主要包括勤奋、勇敢、谦虚、节俭、慎独、智慧、恒心、诚实、守信等。

Personal morality refers to the individual moral awareness and habits and behaviors formed through conscious moral cultivation and social moral education, which is the foundation of other moralities. Personal virtue in traditional Chinese virtues has many aspects, mainly including diligence, courageousness, modesty, thrift, self-restraint, wisdom, perseverance, integrity and credit.

> 勤奋

中国人自古以来就崇尚勤奋。早在远古时代，中华民族的祖先就用勤劳的双手改善生活、创造文明，并以“勤能补拙”来训诫后人。东汉天文学家张衡曾说：“人生在勤，不索何获。”意思就是人生应该勤奋地求索，才会有所收获。中国有许多关于勤奋的俗语，如“一生之计在于勤”“书山有路勤为径”“业精于勤而荒于嬉”等。

中国古代有许多关于勤奋读书的成语故事，如映雪囊萤、悬梁刺股等。

晋代有一个青年叫孙康，家境非常贫寒。孙康读书十分勤奋，但没有钱买灯油，所以晚上无法看书。一天，孙康深夜醒来，看到窗缝里透进了一丝光亮。他打开窗

> Diligence

Chinese believed in hardworking since ancient times. As early as in ancient times, ancestors of the Chinese nation used their hands to improve life and create civilization, and admonished descendants with the saying of hardworking compensating for capacity deficiency. The astronomer Zhang Heng in the Eastern Han Dynasty once said that life should be diligent and no harvest without seeding. China has many common sayings about diligence, e.g. "livelihood of life lies in diligence", "there is no royal road to learning", "achievement is founded on diligence and wasted upon recklessness", etc.

There are a lot of stories about diligent study in ancient China, such as reading under the light of snow reflection and fire ies in a bag and tying one's hair

建筑浮雕“车胤囊萤”（图片提供：FOTOE）
Relief "Che Yin Capsuling Firefly"

一看，原来是地面的积雪映出来的光。孙康激动万分，马上把书拿出来看。读了一会儿，孙康的手脚都冻僵了，他就回屋里跑一跑，暖和了再出去看书。此后，每当有积雪的夜晚，孙康就都会借光读书。若干年后，孙康终于成为饱学之士，成为国家栋梁。晋代还有一个贫穷的青年叫车胤，自幼勤奋好学，但没有多余的钱买灯油。一个夏天的晚上，车胤正在院子里背诗，忽然

on the house beam and jab one's thigh with an awl to keep oneself awake, all about painstaking in one's study.

In the Jin Dynasty, there was a young man named Sun Kang, whose family was very poor. Sun Kang studied very hard, but did not have the money to buy lamp-oil, so at night he was unable to read a book. One day, Sun Kang woke up at night to see a ray of light from the window crack. He opened the window to see light reflected by the snow. Sun Kang was very excited and took out book to read immediately. After a while, Sun Kang's hands and feet were frozen, so he went back into the house to get warm. When he felt warm all over again, he went out to continue the reading. Since then, whenever there was snow night, Sun Kang would read by the light of snow. Several years later, Sun Kang had finally become a man of letters. In the Jin Dynasty, there was also a poor young man named Che Yin. He was studious, but had no extra money to buy lamp-oil. One summer night, Che Yin was reciting a poem in the yard. Suddenly he

看到很多萤火虫在空中飞舞，一时间照亮了院子。车胤心想，若能把这些萤火虫集中在一起，不就相当于一盏灯了吗？于是，他抓了数十只萤火虫放在一个白色的布口袋里，再把它吊在屋里，果然能发出微弱的光亮。此后，车胤就每晚在这盏“灯”下勤学苦读，终于有所成就。这便是“映雪囊萤”成语的由来。

汉代有一个年轻人叫孙敬，读书十分刻苦。如果他在深夜里读书读得困倦，便用绳子一头绑在自己

saw many fireflies fluttering in the air, which at once illuminated the yard. Che Yin thought if he could put these fireflies together, there would be light. He put dozens of fireflies in a white cloth bag, and then hung it in the room, so it could emit faint light. Since then, Che Yin diligently studied under this lamp every night, and finally made it. This was the origin of the idiom of snow reflection and fireflies in a bag.

In the Han Dynasty, there was a young man called Sun Jing who studied very hard. If he felt sleepy deep at night, he would tie one end of the rope with his hair, and the other end to a beam. Once Sun Jing was taking a nap, his head bent down. The rope would pull his hair and his scalp, so he would wake up, and went on reading. Sun Jing studied hard day after day and year after year, finally became a big scholar who thoroughly understood the past and present. Su Qin (?-284 B.C.) was a famous political strategist during the Warring States Period, who held great ambitions when he was young. He used to lobby the king

• 头悬梁
Tie One's Hair on the House Beam

的头发上，另一头绑在房梁上。一旦孙敬打盹，头垂了下去，绳子就会拽住头发，扯疼头皮，他就会清醒过来，接着读书。孙敬日复一日、年复一年地刻苦读书，终于成为一名通晓古今的大学问家。苏秦（？—前284年）是战国时著名的纵横家，年幼时便立下大志，曾游说秦惠王，但未被采纳。苏秦花光了钱财，衣衫褴褛地回到家中，下决心继续勤奋读书。每当深夜读书想要睡觉时，他便用锥子往自己的大腿上刺，让疼痛使自己清醒过来。一年后，苏秦再次周游列国，终于成功说服齐、楚、燕、韩、赵、魏联合抗秦。这便是悬梁刺股成语的由来。

王羲之（321—379年）是东晋著名书法家，被尊为“书圣”。他

of Qin, but he was not accepted. He spent all the money, shabby and destitute, yet determined to continue to study hard. When reading at night, to not fall asleep, he kept his awl pressed to stab himself in the thigh, and let pain sober himself up. A year later, he once again traveled through all the kingdoms, and finally persuaded Qi, Chu, Yan, Han, Zhao and Wei to unite against Qin. This was the origin of the idiom of hair to the beam and needle in the thigh.

Wang Xizhi (321-379) is a famous calligrapher in the Eastern Jin

• **浙江绍兴兰亭鹅池碑亭**

相传王羲之非常喜爱鹅，便在兰亭建造了一口池塘来养鹅，取名“鹅池”。池边建有碑亭，上刻“鹅池”二字。

Pavilion of Lanting Goose Pond in Shaoxing, Zhejiang Province

Legend has it that Wang Xizhi was very fond of goose, and constructed a pond to raise the goose in Lanting, naming it goose pond. There is a stele by the pond, two characters (goose pond) engraved on the stele.

《奉橘帖》（东晋 王羲之）
Calligraphy *Presenting Orange*, by Wang Xizhi (Eastern Jin Dynasty)

的《兰亭序》被誉为“天下第一行书”，一直影响至今。王羲之的书法精绝，不仅缘于他的天赋，更是因为他的勤奋。民间自古便流传有王羲之“墨池”的故事。江西省临川县有一个小池塘，相传王羲之自幼在这附近居住，并每日坚持学习书法。王羲之每次写完字都会去这个小池塘洗笔，时间一长，小池塘的水都被墨水染黑了，因此人称

Dynasty, and is honored as the supreme calligrapher. His *Orchid Pavilion Preface* is known as the best in all cursive handwritings, which has influence far and wide. Wang Xizhi's calligraphy is exquisite, not only because of his genius, but also because of his hard work. The story of Wang Xizhi's inkwell has been told since ancient times. There is a small pond in Linchuan County of Jiangxi Province. According to legend, Wang

“墨池”，又称“洗砚池”。

刘勰（约465—约532年）是南北朝时期著名的文学理论家，他的《文心雕龙》至今仍是中国文学理论的经典作品。刘勰小时候由于家庭条件不好，一直寄居在寺庙中。每天深夜，全寺的僧人都睡觉了，而刘勰却跑到大殿借着灯光读书，有时还会情不自禁地念出声来。有一次，几个僧人听到大殿有读书之声，以为闹鬼，于是就前去捉鬼。到了大殿，他们才发现原来是刘勰在这里读书。

Xizhi lives nearby it since childhood, and every day persists in pratising calligraphy. Every time Wang Xizhi writes words, he will go to the pond to wash the writing brush. After a long time, the small pond water turned to black, so it is called inkwell, also called inkstone washing pond.

Liu Xie (approx. 465-approx. 532) is a famous literary theorist during the Northern and Southern dynasties, his *Wenxin Diaolong* (*Carving a Loong at the Core of Literature*) has been the classical work of Chinese literary theory. When Liu Xie was a child, because of poor family conditions, he had been living in a temple. Late every night, all temple monks were asleep, but Liu Xie went to the main hall reading by light, and sometimes he could not help but read it aloud. Once, several monks heard the sound of reading from the main hall, they thought it was haunted, so they went to seize the ghost. When they got there, they found out it was Liu Xie reading there.

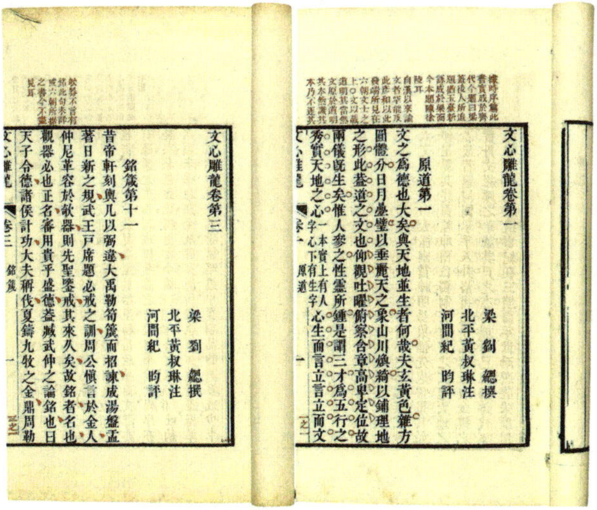

《文心雕龙》书影
Photocopy of *Wenxin Diaolong*

> 勇敢

勇敢就是要敢为人先，敢于面对挑战。中国古代对于勇敢的评价非常高，把它看成是个人的重要美德。孔子曰："勇者不惧。"意思是只有勇敢的人才不惧怕恶劣的环境和险恶的处境。中国自古就有很多大勇之人，他们为了民族和国家的利益，敢于迎难而上，克服重重困难，甚至不惜牺牲自己的生命。

秋瑾（1875—1907年）是中国近代的民主革命志士，幼时曾随兄在私塾读书，因此学识广博，且会骑马击剑。1904年，秋瑾赴日本留学。在日本期间，秋瑾积极参加留日学生的革命活动，并在回国后组织众多革命志士发动武装起义，反对封建旧制。1907年，秋瑾不幸被捕。面对敌人的威逼利诱和严刑拷打，秋瑾毫不动摇，最终英勇就义。

> Courageousness

Being courage is to dare to be pioneers, and dare to face challenges. The ancient Chinese held high regard for the brave, considering it as the important personal virtue. Confucius said the courageous were free from fear, meaning only brave people were not afraid of harsh environment and dangerous situation. China has had many intrepid people since ancient times. For the sake of the interests of the nation and the country, they dare to face up challenges, overcome numerous difficulties, and even sacrifice their lives.

Qiu Jin (1875-1907) was a fighter of democratic revolution in modern China. She studied with her brother in a private school, so had a broad range of knowledge, and was good at horse-riding and fencing. In 1904, she went to study in Japan and took an active part in the revolutionary activities of Chinese students studying

• 秋瑾故居中的秋瑾蜡像

Wax Statue of Qiu Jin in Her Former Residence

in Japan. After returning, she organized many revolutionaries to launch an armed uprising against the feudal system. She was arrested in 1907. Facing the enemies' coercion and torture, Qiu Jin was unshaken in her conviction and was executed.

过零丁洋（文天祥）

辛苦遭逢起一经，干戈寥落四周星。

山河破碎风飘絮，身世浮沉雨打萍。

惶恐滩头说惶恐，零丁洋里叹零丁。

人生自古谁无死？留取丹心照汗青。

回想我早年历尽辛苦，进入仕途，从率领义军抗敌以来，经历了四年的艰苦岁月。

祖国的大好河山在敌军的铁蹄下支离破碎，自己也如此落魄。

想到之前的兵败，我军惶恐撤离的情景，至今还让人心惊；想到去年我军全军覆没，自己被俘，如今漂泊在零丁洋中，只能悲叹自己的孤苦。

人生在世，谁没有一死呢？就让我为国捐躯，留下这颗赤诚之心，光照青史吧！

Too Lonely Ocean (Wen Tianxiang)

Recall that I experienced long labors, entered the official career.

Since leading troops fighting against enemy, I have experienced four difficult years.

The beautiful motherland rivers and mountains, under the oppression of the enemy.

Torn to pieces, I myself also so go down in the world.

Think of the defeat before, horrifying scenes of our army's evacuation still give a person fear;

Think of the whole army was wiped out last year, and I was captured.

Now I drift in the Lingding ocean and can only sigh over my lonliness.

Live in the world, who did not die?

Let me die for my country; leave my sincere heart to light in history!

> 谦虚

中华民族自古就是一个尚谦的民族，不主张扬，在待人处事上讲求中庸，善于自我节制。在中国古代著名的哲学书籍《周易》中，几乎所有的卦象都有好有坏，而独有"谦卦"全部是好的，可见古人对于谦虚的崇尚。一般有大成就的人都很谦虚，懂得"山外有山，人外有人"的道理。

孔子有句名言："三人行必有我师焉。"尽管他的学问很深，但

> Modesty

The Chinese nation is a nation advocating modesty and self-effacement. They emphasize the doctrine of the mean in treating people and handling matters, and are good at self-control. In the famous

• **山东曲阜孔庙**

孔庙是纪念和祭祀孔子的祠庙建筑，分布于全国各地，至今保存较好的仍有数百座。位于山东曲阜的孔庙于1994年被列入世界文化遗产名录。

Confucius Temple in Qufu, Shandong Province

Confucius Temples are ancestral architecture for memorial and worship of Confucius, located in many parts of the country. Hundreds of them are well preserved. In 1994, the Confucius Temple in Qufu, Shandong is included into the list of World Cultural Heritage.

《周易》

《周易》亦称《易经》，是中国古代一部描述事物变化规律的哲学著作，距今已有三千多年的历史。《周易》囊括了天文、地理、军事、科学、文学、农业等丰富的知识内容，讲究阴阳相生相克、刚柔并济，提倡自强不息、厚德载物。《周易》在中国传统文化中占有重要地位，古代帝王用以施政，百姓则用以占卜事象。

Zhouyi (*Book of Changes*)

Zhouyi also known as *Yi Jing* (*The Book of Changes*) in China, which is a philosophy work describing the law of changes of things in ancient China, having a history of over 3000 years. *Zhouyi* includes abundant knowledge, such as astronomy, geography, military affairs, science, literature, agriculture, etc., paying attention to Yin and Yang and coupling hardness with softness. It advocates unremitting self-improvement and the eclectic great virtue. *Zhouyi* occupies an important position in traditional Chinese culture. The ancient emperors used *Zhouyi* for administration and the people used it to divine things.

• 《周易》古书影

Copy of Ancient Book *Zhouyi*

依然非常谦虚。民间流传有这样一个故事：孔子周游列国的时候，有一天驾车去晋国。路上他看见一个小孩在路中央堆了很多碎石和瓦片

ancient Chinese philosophy book *Zhouyi*, almost all of the trigrams are both good and bad, but only modest trigrams are all good. We can see that the ancients advocate for modesty. In general, people

挡住了去路，于是上前询问原因。小孩指着地上的碎石和瓦片问："您看这是什么呢？"孔子低头一看，说这好像是一座城池。小孩子点点头说："既然是座城，那么应该是城给车让路还是车给城让路呢？我再考考您——鹅的叫声为什么大？"孔子答道："因为鹅的脖子很长，所以叫声大。"孩子反问道："那为什么青蛙的脖子很短，可是叫声也很大呢？"孔子被问住了，无言以对，于是笑着对自己的学生说："我不如他啊，他可以做我的老师了。"

白居易（772—846年）是唐代著名的政治家和诗人，为人非常谦虚，注意让自己的诗尽量通俗易懂。他每写完一首诗，总是念给不识字的百姓们听。如果他们听不懂，白居易就会虚心请教，再回去修改；改后再读给这些人听，直到他们能听懂为止。中国有句话叫"君子学于圣人，圣人学于民"。白居易之所以创造出了许多脍炙人口的诗文，其中一个重要的原因就是他能虚心向普通老百姓学习。

梅兰芳（1894—1961年）是中国近代著名的京剧表演艺术家。尽

• 白居易像
Portrait of Bai Juyi

who succeed are very modest. They understand the truth—there's always someone more capable than us.

Confucius said, "Whenever I walk with two other men, I can always find teachers in them." Despite his deep knowledge, he was still very modest. A tale said that when Confucius traveled through all the kingdoms, one day on the way to the state of Jin he saw a child piling up many crushed stones and gravels in the way. He asked for the reason. The child pointed at the

管他的艺术水平很高，但依然虚心接受别人的意见。戏曲理论家齐如山曾在观看了梅兰芳的戏之后，给他写信指出哪里演得不对。梅兰芳不但虚心接受，还因此与齐如山建立起了深厚的友谊。不仅如此，梅兰芳还虚心向普通人请教。有一次，梅兰芳演出京剧《杀惜》，虽然博得了观众的喝彩声，但他却听见有一位老者说 “不好” 。演戏结束后，梅兰芳来不及卸装就把这位老人接到家中，恭恭敬敬地向老人请教：“刚才听到老人家说我的戏

京剧《贵妃醉酒》中的梅兰芳

Mei Lanfang in Beijing Opera *Drunken Concubine*

stones and gravels on the ground and asked, "What do you think are these"? Confucius looked down and said it looked like a city. The children nodded and said, "Since it is a city, should the city give way to the chariot or the chariot makes way for the city? Let me ask you another question—why the gooses quack so loud?" Confucius replied, "Because gooses have long necks." The child asked again, "Frogs barely having necks, how come they croak so noisy as well?" Confucius was stumped, with nothing to say in reply. He smiled at his students and said, "He knows more than I do; he can be my teacher."

Bai Juyi (772-846), a famous statesman and poet of the Tang Dynasty, every time wrote a poem, he always read it to the illiterate people. If they didn't understand, Bai Juyi would rewrite it and went back to read for those people again until they could understand. There is a saying in China, "Gentleman learns from Saint, and Saint learns from people." Bai Juyi left so many popular poems, and one

不好，说我戏不好的人就是我的老师。先生说不好，必有高见，学生定请赐教。”老人看见梅兰芳如此谦虚，于是指出：“主人公上楼和下楼的台步，按梨园规定应是上七下八，你为什么要八上八下？”梅兰芳意识到自己表演上的疏忽，于是连声称谢，并且从此作了纠正。

徐悲鸿（1895—1953年）是中国近代著名的画家，早年留学法国，回国之后致力于中西绘画的融合。徐悲鸿的画深深影响了几代人，可谓一代绘画大师。但他为人却非常谦虚，总能听取别人的意见。有一次他举办画展，参观者都

of the important reasons is that he could learn from the ordinary people and made his poems quite easy to understand.

Mei Lanfang (1894-1961), the most famous Beijing Opera performer in modern China, despite his great artistic achievement, he was willing to listen to people's opinions with an open mind. Opera theorist Qi Rushan once wrote to him after watching Mei Lanfang's performance some criticism. Mei Lanfang not only accepted his idea, also established a profound friendship with Qi Rushan. Moreover, Mei Lanfang also humbly asked people for advice. Once, Mei Lanfang performed the Beijing Opera called *Kill Xi*. Among loud bravoes, he heard an old man said "it's no good". As soon as Mei Lanfang got off the stage, he invited the old man to his home before he could clean up make-ups. He said respectfully to the old man, "Just now I heard you said that my performance was not good enough. I regard those who criticize me as my teachers. Sir, will you enlighten me please? " Moved by Mei Lanfang's

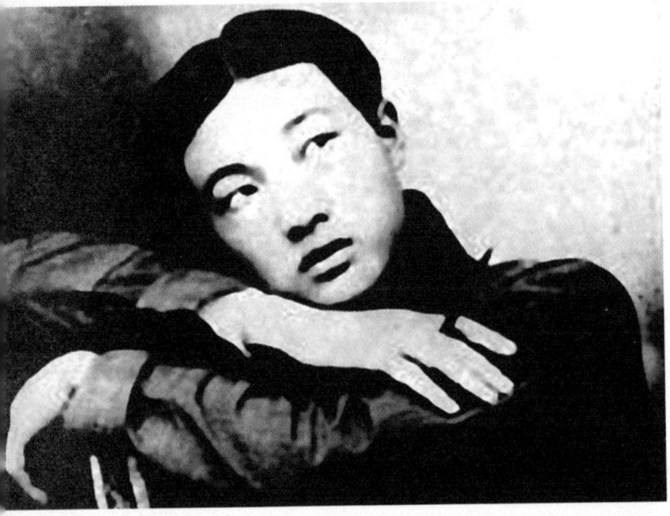

• 徐悲鸿像
Portrait of Xu Beihong

• 《骏马图》（徐悲鸿）
Horse, by Xu Beihong

说极好，但其中一位老农却指着一幅画对他说：“先生，您这幅画里的鸭子画错了。您画的是麻鸭，可是麻鸭尾巴哪有那么长的？”原来，徐悲鸿展出的一幅《写东坡春江水暖诗意》画作，所画的麻鸭尾巴确实很长，与事实不符。徐悲鸿高兴地接受了老农的批评，并向老农表达深深的谢意，之后很快对这幅画作了修改。

modesty, the old man said, "According to the rules, the leading character goes upstairs seven steps and downstairs eight steps on the stage, but what you did was eight up and eight down." Mei Lanfang realized his negligence and never made the mistake since then. He expressed his thanks to the old man sincerely.

Xu Beihong (1895-1953), one of the most famous Chinese painters in modern time, studied in France when he was young and devoted to the integration of Chinese and Western painting styles when he came back to China. His paintings deeply influenced several generations and he was a great artist in his time. He was also a modest man and valued criticism from viewers very much. Once a farmer pointed at one painting in exhibition and said to him, "Sir, you made a mistake. A sheldrake couldn't have such a long tail." Xu Beihong realized the farmer was correct and soon repainted the sheldrake's tail in his painting *Writing the Poetic Sentiment of Dongpo's Warm Spring River*.

> 节俭

中国人自古便提倡节俭。《朱子家训》中云："一粥一饭，当思来处不易；半丝半缕，恒念物力维艰。"意思是吃饭的时候要想到，一碗粥、一碗饭都来之不易，不能轻易浪费；穿衣的时候，要想到每一缕布都来之不易，也不能轻易

• 明代"朱子家训"墨

The Ink Stick of "Zhuzi Parental Instruction" Made in the Ming Dynasty

> Thrift

The habit of thrift has been encouraged by Chinese since ancient times. It is said in *Zhuzi Parental Instruction* "when eating, think of every rice not easily got; when dressing, think of every thread not easily made." Thrift means not greedy, only modest gains, and no extravagance and waste. Chinese people often say thrift helps develop a hard-working character, and extravagance makes people greedy. People are easy to become greedy, demand things that one should not have and lose moral compass.

Ji Wenzi (?-568 B.C.) was a famous diplomat and politician of State Lu in

《朱子家训》

《朱子家训》是一部以家庭道德为主的启蒙教材，作者是明末清初的学者朱柏庐（1627—1698年）。全书仅522字，以名言警句作为表达方式，方便口头传训，也可以写成对联、条幅等张贴在室内，被历代士大夫尊为“治家之经”。《朱子家训》从治家的角度谈了安全、勤俭、婚姻、教育、谦和、交友、自省、向善等各个方面的问题，精辟地阐明了修身治家之道，教导人们做一个光明磊落、知书达理、宽容善良的人，这也是中国传统文化的一贯追求。

Zhuzi Parental Instruction

Zhuzi Parental Instruction is an enlightenment teaching material based on the family moral, authored by the scholar Zhu Bailu (1627-1698) during the late Ming Dynasty and early Qing Dynasty. It contains only 522 words, using aphorism for lessons, which is convenient to convey, and can be written as a poetic couplet and posted in the room. It is revered as the canon of managing the household by literati. *Zhuzi Parental Instruction*, from a point of view of managing the household, discusses all aspects of everyday life such as security, thrift, marriage, education, modesty, making friends, self-communion and learning virtue, brilliantly expounds the way of practicing moral culture and teaches people to be an aboveboard, educated, reasonable, tolerant and kind, and this is also the consistent pursuit of Chinese traditional culture.

• “朱熹家训”屏风

A Screen Inscribed with "Family Precepts by Zhu Xi"

浪费。节俭意味着不贪婪，只适度地获取，不铺张浪费。中国人常说“俭以养德”，意思是节俭有助于养成质朴勤劳的品德，而浪费铺张则容易使个人欲望膨胀，人就容易变得贪婪，索取不应该拥有的东西，丧失掉美好的品德。

季文子（？—前568年）是春秋时期鲁国的贵族，著名的外交家和政治家，虽然身居高位，但却极其节俭，并且严格要求家人也过俭朴的生活。除了朝服以外，他很少穿华贵的衣服，乘坐的车马也非常简朴。百官看到季文子非常简朴，都很敬重他，但也有人劝他：“你身为上卿，德高望重，但却如此不注重服饰、车马，别人会觉得你过于寒酸。而且你出使到别的国家，别国的人也可能会笑话你。所以希望你能够注意一下自己的服饰，我们国家才有体面。”季文子听后说：“你说的确实有道理，但每当我看见老百姓还穿不上衣服、吃不上饭的时候，就感到很难过。所以我自己坚持过与百姓类似的生活，也不允许我的家里人太奢侈。当然，出使到别的国家的时候，我会注意一

the Spring and Autumn Period. Born in noble family and being a high ranking official for more than 30 years, Ji Wenzi was rich, but lived an extremely frugal life. He also asked his family to do so. He always wore plain clothes in daily life and rode in a very simple carriage. His thrift earned him lots of respect from other officials. Someone tried to persuade him, "You are a minister, noble character and high prestige, so you should be more fastidious about your clothing, or people would laugh at your shabbiness. And to keep the dignity of our state is your obligation." Ji Wenzi replied, "Thank you for your advice. But I feel sorry for our people whenever I see that they don't have enough to wear and eat sometimes. So I and my family insist on the life similar to common people. Of course, I will be well dressed when I am sent on a diplomatic mission abroad. To judge a diplomat is not by his clothes and carriage, but mainly by his moral integrity. I believe I excel in virtue, without any contempt." By the example of Ji Wenzi, most of Lu State officials were very thrifty.

Liu Yan, an official of the Tang Dynasty who was good at financial management and administration. He was

下服饰的。但是评判一个外交官的好坏，并不是看他的服饰和车马，而主要是看他的德行。我非常注重修德行，即使服饰上差一些，相信别国人也不会嘲笑我们国家的。”由于季文子的榜样作用，鲁国的官员们大都非常节俭。

刘晏是唐代的官员，善于理财，在行政上也非常有才干，因此受到唐肃宗、唐代宗两代皇帝的重用，负责掌管国家的财政大权。可是刘晏在日常生活中却十分节俭，而且要求他的妻子和子女们也都力行节俭。刘晏的住宅坐落在长安（今陕西省西安市）的一个小巷里，外表和内部装修都和普通百姓家一样，没有雕梁画栋，更没有亭台楼阁，屋里陈设也非常简单。他的饮食也很简朴，民间曾流传他有时上朝就随身带两个烧饼当做早餐，家里的家务事都是妻子、儿女自己动手做，没有多少佣人。刘晏常对家人和朋友说，居所但求能够躲避风雨，何必富丽堂皇；饮食只要能够吃饱喝足，何必讲究精美；车马只求代步即可，何必非要骏马、豪车？

• 刘晏雕像（图片提供：FOTOE）
Statue of Liu Yan

appointed to an important position by Emperor Suzong and Emperor Daizong in the Tang Dynasty. He administered finances of the state but lived a very thrifty life. Liu Yan's house was located in an alley in Chang'an (today's Xi'an City, Shaanxi Province). It was not much different from houses of ordinary people. There were no pavilions and terraces in the yard. It was a plainly furnished house without rich ornament. He and his

朱元璋（1328—1398年）是明朝的开国皇帝，他从小生活困苦，注重节俭，当上皇帝后也过着俭朴的生活。明朝建立不久，朱元璋便发现达官贵人穷奢极欲，过着花天酒地的生活，于是决心要整治官场奢侈的风气。有一次，皇后过生日，文武官员都来贺寿，带了各种各样的珍贵礼物。宴客时，朱元

• 明太祖朱元璋像

Portrait of Zhu Yuanzhang, the First Emperor of the Ming Dynasty

family ate simple food every day. He always went to court with two sesame seed cakes for breakfast. His wife and children did most chores. Liu Yan often told his family and friends that a house which could shelter you from wind and rain is good enough, magnificence is not necessary; diet which could keep you from starving is satisfying, delicacies is not necessary; carriage which could bring you to your destination is alright, fine horses are not necessary...

Zhu Yuanzhang (1328-1398), the founding emperor of the Ming Dynasty, lived a poor life since childhood. So he advocated thrifty, and kept this lifestyle even after he became an emperor. Shortly after the Ming Dynasty was established, Zhu Yuanzhang found that high officials and noble lords were very extravagant, living a luxurious life, so he determined to change their luxurious behavior. Once on the empress's birthday, civil and military officials came to celebrate, bringing with various precious gifts. In the celebration, Zhu Yuanzhang asked several ministers to stay for dinner, which has just four dishes, namely, fried radish, fried leeks, two big plates of vegetables as well as Tofu soup with chopped scallion pieces. The ministers

- **明代紫砂壶**

明代社会尚俭，在这种风气的影响下，建筑、家具和生活用品等都设计简约。

Purple Clay Tea Pot Made in the Ming Dynasty

The Ming Dynasty social convention was thrifty. Under this atmosphere, the building, furniture and daily necessities were brief designed.

璋让几个大臣留下吃饭，并吩咐上菜。这顿饭一共只上了四道菜：炒萝卜、炒韭菜、两大碗青菜和葱花豆腐汤。众大臣都迷惑不解，觉得皇后过生日，普天同庆，应该吃山珍海味才是。朱元璋说：“尽管我们取得了政权，但还是应该做到节俭，不能随便浪费，粗茶淡饭就好了。”大臣们听罢才知道朱元璋的用意。随后，朱元璋当众宣布：“今后众大臣宴请，最多只能四菜一汤，这次宴会即是榜样。若有人违反，一定严惩不贷。”后来，“四菜一汤”的规矩便从宫廷传到民间。

were all very puzzled, because they thought that to celebrate such an occasion as the empress's birthday, nice dishes of every kind must be served. However, Zhu Yuanzhang said, "We should continue to be thrifty and reduce waste although we have built the regime. In this sense, these simple dishes are enough for us." The ministers all got Zhu Yuanzhang's meaning. Afterwards, Zhu Yuanzhang announced to them, "In the future, whenever you hold a banquet, you should only serve no more than four dishes and one soup. Just take today's banquet as an example. Anyone who violates my order will be punished severely." Later, the rule of four dishes and one soup became a model of incorruptible governance and was well adopted.

> 慎独

慎独就是指一个人在独处的时候要具有高度的自觉性，说话做事要谨慎，要遵守道德，不能因为没有别人的监督而做坏事或错事。中国最早的诗歌总集《诗经》曰："不愧于屋漏。"意思是即使一个人在家，也应该注意举头三尺有神明，不能做违法或有碍道德的事。

春秋时期，鲁国有一位宰相名叫公仪休，非常廉洁，从不接受别人的礼物。公仪休有一个爱好，就是非常喜欢吃鱼。所以一些想要巴结他的人知道送金银珠宝一定行不通，便挑选了全国各地的好鱼来送给他，却仍然被挡在了门外。公仪休的弟弟很不理解，问公仪休为什么不收。公仪休说："他们知道我喜欢吃鱼，所以才来投其所好，定

> Self-restraint

Self-restraint means that a person should exercise self-control when he is alone, and should speak and act prudently. He should abide by moral principles, not to do something bad or wrong even when no one is watching. China's first poetry anthology *The Book of Songs* reads, "Be righteous under all circumstances." It means that a person at home alone should notice that the Divine is always there watching him, so he should never do evil and never undermine morality.

During the Spring and Autumn Period (770 B.C.-476 B.C.), there was a prime minister named Gong Yixiu in the state of Lu. He was a man of integrity and never accepted gift. Gong Yixiu liked eating fish, so some people tried to butter him by picking out good fish all over the country and sending to him as a

• 某中学学生表演的《公仪休拒收鲤鱼》（图片提供：FOTOE）
Gong Yixiu Rejecting Carp Performed by Middle School Students

是有所求！鱼虽然不是贵重物品，但我有俸禄，可以用自己的钱去买鱼，何必收别人的礼物，而弄得自己为此担惊受怕呢？”

东汉有一位官员叫杨震，善于发现、举荐人才。他任荆州刺史时，曾发现有一个叫王密的官员才华出众，于是便向朝廷举荐。朝廷接受了杨震的举荐，委任王密担任

gift, because they know that he would not accept gold, silver on jewelry. However, Gong Yixiu still shut the door on them. His brother did not understand, and asked Gong Yixiu why not accept those fish. Gong Yixiu answered, "They know I like eating fish, so they give me what I desire for in a hope to get some favors from me! Although fish are not qualified as bribes, I have a salary, and I can afford to buy

朝中要职。王密听说是杨震举荐之后十分感激，带了十两黄金私下拜会杨震以表谢意，不料杨震执意不收。王密劝道："现在是深夜，没有人知道。"杨震听后十分震怒，斥责道："我本觉得你有才华，才举荐你，并不是希望你能送我礼物和金钱。虽然这是在夜里，但天知、神知、我知、你知，怎么会没人知道！"杨震一席话说得王密非常羞愧，于是急忙起身谢罪，拿着黄金走了。此后，他对杨震更加敬重了。

• 杨震像

Portrait of Yang Zhen

fish with my own money. So why accept those fish and make myself worried about it? "

There was an official in the Eastern Han Dynasty (25-220) named Yang Zhen, who was good at discovering and recommending talents. When he served as the governor of Jingzhou, he found that an official named Wang Mi was more competent than others, so he recommended Wang Mi to the court. The court accepted Yang Zhen's recommendation, and appointed Wang Mi to an important position in the central government. Knowing that it was Yang Zhen who recommended him, Wang Mi was very grateful, he took 10 Liang (a unit of weight in China) of gold to thank Yang Zhen in private. Unexpectedly, Yang Zhen insisted on not accepting the gold. Wang Mi then tried to talk him over, "Now it is late at night, nobody knows." Hearing this, Yang Zhen was furious and scolded Wang Mi, "The reason why I recommended you is that I thought you were talented. I didn't do that for your gifts and money. Although it is late at night, heaven knows, God knows, I know and you know. How can you say nobody knows?" What Yang

• 曾国藩像
Portrait of Zeng Guofan

曾国藩（1811—1872年）是清代名臣，曾辅佐皇帝实现了清代中兴。曾国藩非常强调慎独，他年轻时便给自己制定了一个规矩：每天晚上都不出去应酬，而是静坐半个小时，思索一下今日所做的事是对是错，有无不恰当之处，有无需要改正之处。后来直至功成名就，他在独处的时候仍以反思和读书为主。

Zhen said made Wang Mi very ashamed, therefore he stood up to apologize hurriedly, and took his gold back. Since then, he held Yang Zhen in more respect.

Zeng Guofan (1811-1872) was a famous official in the Qing Dynasty (1616-1911), who assisted emperors of the Qing Dynasty to achieve resurgence. He laid great importance on self-restraint. When he was young, he made a rule for himself that every night he would not go out to take part in social activities. Instead, he would sit in tranquility for half an hour to examine whether what he had done that day was right or wrong; whether there was something inappropriate that needed correcting. Even after he achieved success and won recognition, he insisted on spending much time on reading books and examining himself when he was in tranquil solitude.

> 智慧

在中国的诸多美德之中，智慧往往排在前列。智慧其实就是能够根据所了解到的信息，做出正确的判断和选择。智慧往往体现在实践之中，尤其是一个人在面临困难和选择的时候，最能体现智慧的重要性。在政治生活、军事斗争中，智慧显得极其重要。它可以帮助人去应对各种复杂的局面，取得一个又一个胜利。

田单是战国时期齐国的著名将领。公元前284年，燕国大军攻齐，连破七十余城，随后集中兵力围攻即墨（今属山东），齐国危在旦夕。齐王命田单为将，抵抗燕军。田单趁两军相持之际，集结了七千多名兵士，迅速整顿军备，修筑城垒。与此同时，田单用计麻痹燕

> Wisdom

Among many Chinese virtues, wisdom always tops the list. Wisdom is the ability to make correct judgment and decision according to information available. It often shines in actual practice and manifested its importance mostly in situations where a person is in difficulty and has to make decisions. In political life and military combats, wisdom is extremely important, with which one manage to deal with complicated situations and achieve one victory after another.

Tian Dan was a famous general and minister in the state of Qi during the Warring States Period (475 B.C.-221 B.C.). In 284 B.C., Yan's army attacked Qi and captured more than 70 cities one after another. Afterwards the army concentrated forces to besiege Jimo

• 田单像
Portrait of Tian Dan

军。他先命精壮兵士隐伏于城内，让老弱妇孺登城守望；又派使者前往燕营诈降，同时让即墨的富豪纷纷持重金贿赂燕将，假称即墨城破后请保其妻小。这一系列的措施使燕军以为齐军将降，愈加懈怠。田单见反攻的时机已成熟，便找来千余头牛，角上绑着利刃，尾部扎上浸过油的芦苇。一天深夜，田单命人点燃牛尾的芦苇，使得千余头牛负痛狂奔，从城脚预挖的数十条通道直奔燕营。田单再命五千精壮兵士紧随其后，杀入敌营。即墨城

(currently in Shandong Province), driving Qi to the verge of falling. To resist Yan's forces, the king of Qi appointed Tian Dan as the commander of Qi's army. When the war was at a stalemate, Tian Dan gathered more than seven thousand soldiers, quickly reorganizing armament and building fortifications. At the same time, Tian Dan made Yan's army less vigilant with ruses. He first hid strong soldiers in the city, and let the weak ascend the city wall to watch; then he sent messengers to Yan's camps pretending to surrender, meanwhile he asked rich and powerful people of Jimo to bribe Yan's generals with a large sum of gold, pleading for the protection of their wives and children after Jimo was captured. These ruses convinced Yan's army that Qi's troops would surrender so they were more slack. Tian Dan then believed the time for a counterattack was ripe, so he gathered more than 1000 cattle whose horns were strapped with blades and tails tied with oil-impregnated reeds. One late night, Tian Dan ordered to light those reeds on oxtails. More than 1000 cattle, being in pain, ran through dozens of channels pre-excavated from the foot of the city to Yan's camps. Tian Dan then ordered five thousand strong soldiers to

• 田单命人在牛尾上绑芦苇
Tian Dan Ordering People to Tie Reeds on the Oxtails

内，他让余下的军民用力擂鼓、呐喊。燕军听到鼓声，又见无数冒着火的怪物直面扑来，惊慌失措，纷纷夺路逃命。田单亲率精兵乘胜追击，将燕军逐出齐国边境，最后将七十余城全部收回。

诸葛亮（181—234年）是三国时期的蜀汉丞相，杰出的政治家、军事家、发明家、文学家。中国古典名著《三国演义》中曾记载过一篇关于诸葛亮的智谋故事——草船借箭。三国时期，曹操率领魏国大军南下，企图攻克蜀国和吴国。蜀国和吴国联合起来与魏军隔江对抗。当时，箭是非常重要的战略物

follow those cattle into Yan's camps to attack, while in the city of Jimo, the rest of the troops and civilians beat drums forcefully and cried out loud under Tian Dan's order. Hearing the beating of drums and seeing countless cattle rushed toward them with fire, Yan's troops were panic-stricken and rushed to escape. Tian Dan then led troops to pursue the retreating of Yan's army. Finally, he drove Yan's army out of Qi's borders, and took back all the captured cities.

Zhuge Liang (181-234) was the prime minister of the Shu Han regime during the Three Kingdoms Period (220-280). He was an outstanding statesman, military strategist, inventor and writer. The Chinese classic *Romance of the Three Kingdoms* has a story about Zhuge Liang's wisdom: borrowing arrows with thatched boats. During the Three Kingdoms Period, Cao Cao led the Wei

• 诸葛亮像
Portrait of Zhuge Liang

army southward in an attempt to conquer the states of Shu and Wu. To fight against the Wei army, Shu and Wu formed an alliance across the river. However, the alliance of Shu and Wu were short of arrows, the very important weapon at that time. Zhuge Liang then came up with a wonderful idea. He ordered soldiers of Shu to send many boats full of scarecrows to Cao Cao's camps in a foggy day. When these boats were near Cao Cao's camps, Zhuge Liang let soldiers

资，蜀国和吴国都非常匮乏。于是，诸葛亮想出了一个妙计。他让蜀国的士兵在一个大雾天派出很多船，船上绑了许多草人。当这些草船快要驶到曹军营地时，诸葛亮命船上的士兵拼命擂鼓。由于江上的雾太大，魏军不清楚对方到底派出了多少兵力，不敢轻举妄动，只得不断放箭。一时间，箭如大雨一般射到草人身上。待草人身上插满了箭，诸葛亮便命士兵们停止擂鼓，收兵回营。诸葛亮凭借着他的智慧，不费一兵一卒就获得了十万支箭，轻松地解决了战略物资匮乏的问题。

• 草船借箭
Borrowing Arrows with Thatched Boats

• 曹冲称象（图片提供：微图）
Cao Chong Weighing an Elephant

on board beat drums hard. Because of dense fog above the river, the army of Wei did not know how many troops the alliance had sent, so they did not dare to act recklessly but to constantly shot arrows off. Instantly, arrows fell on scarecrows like heavy rain until the scarecrows were full of them. Zhuge Liang then ordered the soldiers to stop beating drums and to retreat back to the camp. With his stratagem, Zhuge Liang obtained one hundred thousand arrows without striking a blow, and easily solved the shortage of weapons.

曹冲（196—208年）是三国时期曹操的儿子。曹冲非常有智慧，曾被称为“神童”，民间流传着很多关于他的故事。有一次，国外的官员送给曹操一头大象。曹操很想知道这头大象到底有多重，就命官员想办法称一称。当时没有能够给象称重的秤，官员们想尽办法都没能做到。这时，曹冲走上前来，叫

Cao Chong (196-208) was the son of Cao Cao in the Three Kingdoms Period (220-280). Cao Chong was so wise that he was once known as a prodigy. There were many stories about him. Once, a foreign official sent Cao Cao an elephant as a gift. Being curious about how heavy the elephant was, Cao Cao asked his officials to tries their best to weigh it. At that time, there was no scale big enough

人牵了大象跟着他到河边去。河边停靠着一艘大船，曹冲命人把大象牵到船上去。大象到了船上，船自然往下沉了一些。曹冲让人在下沉的地方划了一道记号，然后把大象牵上岸。接着，他又命人挑一些石块放到船上，直到船再下沉到标记处。这时只要分别称出这些石块的重量，加起来就是大象的重量了。

司马光（1019—1086年）是宋朝著名的历史学家，他的著作《资治通鉴》是中国的史学巨作，流传至今。司马光小时候就非常有智

to weigh the elephant, the officials were stumped although they had racked their brains. Then Cao Chong came up and asked someone to lead the elephant to follow him to the riverside, along which there was a huge boat. He ordered to lead the elephant to board the boat, afterward the boast sank down a little into the water. Cao Chong then asked people to mark a line at the water line. After the elephant was led ashore, he ordered people to carry some stones into the boat until it sank to where the mark was. Then the weight of the elephant would be clear after weighing all the stones on the boat.

Sima Guang (1019-1086) was a famous historian in the Song Dynasty (960-1279). His book *History as a Mirror* is China's historical masterpiece. Sima Guang was very clever since childhood. Once, when he played together with many children, one of them climbed on a vat full of water, and accidentally fell into it. While other children cried, Sima Guang was the only one who kept very calm. Seeing a big stone in front of him

• 司马光像
Portrait of Sima Guang

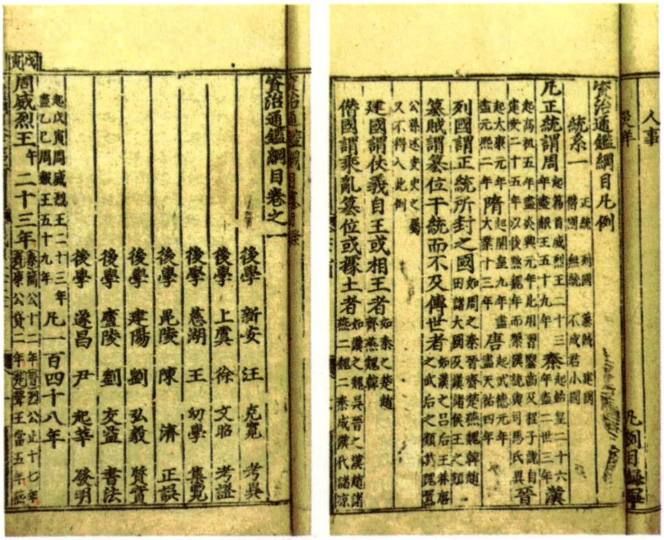
資治通鑑綱目卷之一
後學 新安 汪克寬 考異
後學 上虞 徐文昭 考證
後學 慈湖 王幼學 集覽
後學 武陵 陳濟 正誤
後學 建陽 劉弘毅 贊實
後學 廬陵 劉友益 書法
後學 遂昌 尹起莘 發明
周威烈王二十三年

資治通鑑綱目凡例
統系一
凡正統謂周秦漢晉隋唐
列國謂正統所封之國
篡賊謂篡位干統而不及傳世者
建國謂仗義自王或相王者
僭國謂乘亂篡位或據土者

• 《资治通鉴》书影
Photocopy of *History as a Mirror*

慧。有一次，司马光和很多小孩在一起玩耍。一个小孩爬到了一个盛满了水的大缸上，不小心一头栽了进去。孩子们都束手无策，着急地哭了起来，唯有司马光非常镇定。他看见前面有一块大石头，便赶快搬起石头砸破了大缸。缸破了，水流了出来，掉进缸里的小孩顺利脱险。这就是中国人耳熟能详的“司马光砸缸”的故事。

he quickly lifted it to break the vat. After the vat was broken and the water inside owed out, the child in it was saved. This is the story of Sima Guang Breaking the Vat, which is well known by Chinese.

> 恒心

中国有句古话“靡不有初，鲜克有终”，意思是做事没有人不肯善始，但很少有人能善终。很多人做事都有一个很好的开始，但很少有人能够坚持到最后。孟子曰：“苟无恒心，放辟邪侈，无不为已。”意思是如果一个人没有恒心，就会屡屡纵容自己，最终一事无成。

中国民间流传着“愚公移山”的故事。古时候有一个老头，大家都称他为“愚公”。愚公所住的村子前面有两座大山，村民们每次出门都很不方便，要绕很远的路。愚公下定决心要把这两座山移走。于是，他率领家人每天用锄头挖走山上的土和石块，再背到很远的地方去。开始，亲朋好友听说愚公想

> Perseverance

There is an old saying in China that "Few people fail to have a good start in doing something, yet fewer people can finish it." It means that many people manage to have a good start in doing something, but very few people have perseverance and persistence to finish it. Mencius also said that "without perseverance, one will act wrong and achieve nothing". Namely, if a person has no perseverance, he would often indulge himself and end up achieving nothing.

In Chinese folklore there is a story about the Foolish Old Man who tried to remove the mountains. In ancient times there was an old man who was called the Foolish Old Man. In front of the village he lived in, there were two huge mountains that made villagers' traffic very inconvenient. Villagers had

要用这种方法把山移走，都觉得十分可笑。但愚公却依然坚持，说："我们这几个人可能搬不走这两座大山，但我还有儿子，儿子还会有孙子，子子孙孙是没有穷尽的，只要坚持不懈，两座山终究会被凿平。"后来天帝被愚公的精神感动了，便派天神将山挪走了。

to go around the mountains every time they went out. The Foolish Old Man then was determined to remove the two mountains away, so he led his family to dig soil and stone out of the mountains with hoes, and to carry them on their back to places far away. Hearing that the Foolish Old Man intended to remove the mountains in such ways, his friends and relatives all thought it ridiculous. The Foolish Old Man, however, insisted and said, "A few of us possibly cannot move these two mountains away, but I have my sons and my sons are going to have grandsons. There will be descendants generation after generation. As long as we have perseverance, the two mountains will eventually be removed." Later, the deity was moved by the Foolish Old Man's spirit, and sent help to move the mountains away.

There is an old saying in China that "with time and perseverance, iron bars would be filed to needles (Nothing is difficult if you put your heart into it)." It

• 根雕《愚公移山》
Root Carving: *The Foolish Old Man Removing the Mountains*

李白像

Portrait of Li Bai

中国有句老话："只要功夫深，铁杵磨成针。"讲的是唐代著名大诗人李白（701—762年）的故事。相传李白小时候不喜欢读书，每天读一两个时辰就不耐烦了。有一次，李白外出时看见一个老婆婆在河边磨一根铁棒，十分好奇，便问老婆婆在做什么。老婆婆回答说她想把这根铁棒磨成一根绣花针。李白听后哈哈大笑说："这怎么可能！这根铁棒如此粗大，怎么能磨成细细的绣花针呢？"老婆婆却不以为然："只要有恒心，每天坚持磨，肯定可以做到。"听到老婆婆

comes from the story about Li Bai (701-762), a famous poet in the Tang Dynasty (618-907). According to legend, Li Bai did not like studying in his childhood and would get impatient after studying one or two hours every day. Once, he went out and saw an old lady rubbing an iron bar at the riverside. Being curious, he asked the old woman what she was doing. The old woman replied that she was going to rub the iron bar into an embroidery needle. Hearing this, Li Bai laughed and said, "That is impossible! How can a bar as thick as this be rubbed into a thin embroidery needle?" The old lady did not agree, "As long as you have perseverance and persist in rubbing it every day, you can surely make it." Hearing what the old woman had said, Li Bai was suddenly enlightened. He began to study in earnest and persisted to do so every day. Later, he accumulated profound knowledge and became an outstanding poet.

的话，李白忽然明白了，于是开始认真读书，每天都坚持不懈，积累了深厚的学识，后来成为杰出的诗人。

智永和尚是唐代著名的书法家，王羲之的七世孙。智永自幼便爱好书法，曾在永欣寺（位于今

Monk Zhiyong, the 7th-generation descendant of Wang Xizhi (a famous calligrapher), was a famous calligrapher in the Tang Dynasty (618-907). He liked calligraphy since he was a child, and had studied calligraphy in earnest in Yongxin Temple (currently in Shaoxing, Zhejiang Province) for thirty years. Zhiyong studied calligraphy very hard and practiced with perseverance every day without even a day's rest. He prepared a large bamboo basket to collect worn-out writing brushes. After he finished his practice, the worn-out writing brushes he had collected filled as many as five baskets. Later, he finally became a famous calligrapher known far and wide and buried those worn writing brushes together in a place which was called the Tomb of Worn Writing Brushes.

Li Shizhen (1518-1593) was a famous medical expert and pharmacologist in the Ming Dynasty (1368-1644). When he was nearly 40 years old, he began to pick and taste herbs around mountains and in the

• 智永书法作品《千字文》
Zhiyong's Calligraphy: *Thousand Character Classic*

- 退笔冢
Tomb of Worn Writing Brushes

wilderness. Besides, he visited many famous doctors and searched for folk prescriptions with his footprints covering more than half of China. He took 27 years to finish the compilation of the *Compendium of Materia Medica*, which contains a total of 52 volumes, covering 1892 kinds of herbs and more than 11,000 prescriptions. In addition to Chinese herbal medicine, it also covers such fields as biology, chemistry, mineralogy,

浙江绍兴）刻苦学习书法30年。智永学习书法非常刻苦，每天坚持练习，一日不断。他准备了一个大竹篓，把练秃了的毛笔扔进竹篓里。待他习成书法时，笔竟整整装满了五篓。后来，智永终于成为远近闻名的书法家，他将这些秃笔埋在一起，称为“退笔冢”。

李时珍（1518—1593年）是明代著名的医学家、药物学家。年近四十岁时，李时珍开始到各地的深山旷野去采尝草药，遍访名医，搜求民间验方。他走遍了大半个中国，历时27年终于写成了《本草纲目》。《本草纲目》共52卷，载药

- 李时珍蜡像
Waxen Image of Li Shizhen

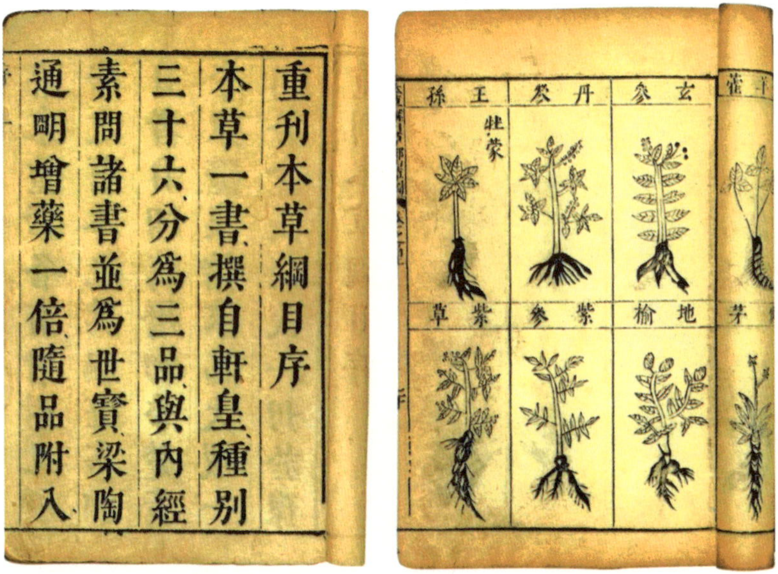
重刊本草綱目序
本草一書撰自軒皇種別
三十六分爲三品與內經
素問諸書並爲世寶梁陶
通明增藥一倍隨品附入

• 《本草纲目》书影
Photocopy of *Compendium of Materia Medica*

1892种、药方11000多个，内容除中草药外，还涉及生物学、化学、矿物学、地质学和天文学等其他领域，被达尔文称赞为“中国古代的百科全书”。正是由于李时珍数十载坚持不懈的努力，才为后世留下了这部旷世巨著。

geology and astronomy, it was praised by Charles Darwin as "Chinese Ancient Encyclopedia". It is owing to Li Shizhen's perseverance for decades that he managed to leave this unrivalled masterpiece for future generations.

> 诚实

诚实是中华民族的美德，儒家经典《中庸》将诚实置于极其高的地位，“诚者，天之道也；思诚者，人之道也。”意思是诚实是自然规律，真诚是做人的规律和基本要求。孟子曰：“人之相识，贵在相知；人之相知，贵在知心。”中国大凡有所成就的人，都具有诚实的美德。

皇甫绩（？—590年）是隋朝著名的大臣。皇甫绩3岁时父亲去世，母亲带着他回到娘家住。他的外公见皇甫绩聪明伶俐，便很重视对他的教育，让他和表兄弟们一起去学堂上学，并对孩子们立下规矩：谁要是无故完不成作业，就按家法重打二十大板。有一天课后，皇甫绩和几个表兄因为下棋忘记了时间，也都忘记做老

> Integrity

Integrity is an important virtue for the Chinese people. In the Confucian classic *The Doctrine of Mean*, integrity is highly praised. The book records that integrity is the law of nature, while sincerity is the law and basic requirements in conducting oneself. As was said by Mencius, "What is precious in people's interaction is mutual understanding, and the most precious in people's mutual understanding is mutual integrity." In China, all people of accomplishment have the virtue of integrity.

Huangfu Ji (? -590) was a famous minister of the Sui Dynasty (581-618). When he lost his father at the age of three, his mother took him back to live with his maternal grandparents. Learning that Huangfu Ji was clever, his grandpa attached great importance to

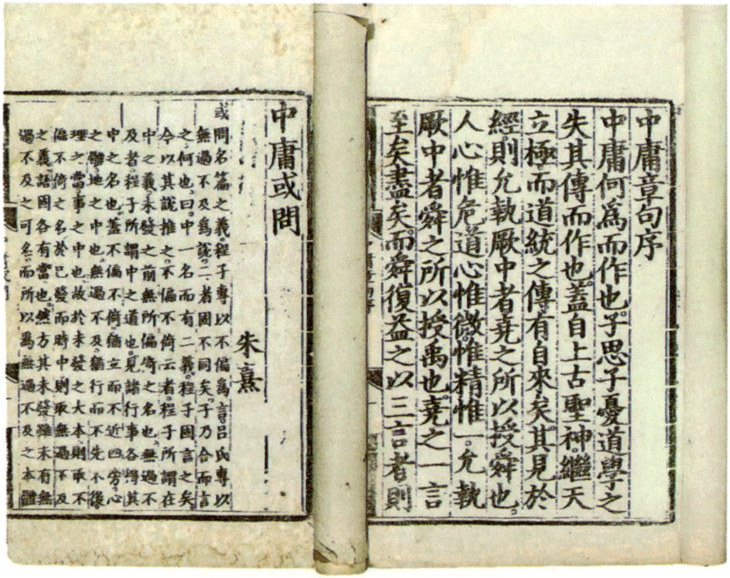
中庸章句序
中庸何爲而作也子思子憂道學之
失其傳而作也蓋自上古聖神繼天
立極而道統之傳有自來矣其見於
經則允執厥中者堯之所以授舜也
人心惟危道心惟微惟精惟一允執
厥中者舜之所以授禹也堯之一言
至矣盡矣而舜復益之以三言者則

中庸或問
朱熹
或問名篇之義程子專以不偏爲言呂氏專以
無過不及爲說二者固不同矣子乃合而言
之何也曰中一名而有二義程子固言之矣
今以其說推之不偏不倚云者程子所謂在
中之義未發之前無所偏倚之名也無過不
及者程子所謂中之道也見諸行事各得其
中之名也蓋不偏不倚猶立而不近四旁心
之體地之中也無過不及猶行而不先不後
理之當事之中也故於未發之大本則取不
偏不倚之名於已發而時中則取無過不及
之義語固各有當也然方其未發雖未有無
過不及之可名而所以爲無過不及之本體

• 《中庸》书影
Photocopy of *The Doctrine of Mean*

师留的作业了。外公知道后，把他们都叫到书房里，先是狠狠地训斥了他们一顿，然后按照规矩，责罚每人重打二十大板。表兄们觉得皇甫绩太小，不忍心看他挨打，于是想为他开脱，可皇甫绩却非常诚实地说下棋是他主动要求的，因此应该和表哥们一起接受责罚。

晏殊（991—1055年）是宋代著名的文学家和政治家。晏殊少年的时候就非常聪明，为人也非常

his education, letting him go to school with his cousins. Besides, the grandpa set a rule for his grandchildren that anyone who failed to finish homework without reason would be given 20 strokes according to the family codes. One day after school, Huangfu Ji and several cousins were so deeply engrossed in playing chess that they forgot to do homework that their teacher had assigned. After knowing this, the grandpa called them all to the study, where they

诚实。14岁那年，皇帝听说他的学识非常出色，便准备了一份试卷来考他。晏殊拿到试卷后，一看题目非常熟悉，前不久刚刚练习过一次，于是就如实向皇帝奏明，请求另外更换考题。皇帝觉得晏殊十分诚实，便赐他“同进士出身”。后来，皇帝想选晏殊当太子的老师，于是来到晏殊家中造访，发现他正

were first given a talking to and then were given 20 strokes in accordance with the rule the grandpa had set. Considering that Huangfu Ji was too young to bear the strokes, the cousins tried to excuse him. But Huangfu Ji confessed with integrity that he was the one who suggested playing chess, hence he should be punished as well with his cousins.

Yan Shu (991-1055) was a famous literati and politician in the Song Dynasty (960-1279). He was a man of integrity and talents since he was young. When Yan Shu was 14, the emperor prepared an examination to test him after getting to know his profound learning. After reading the examination paper, Yan Shu noticed that he was very familiar with the questions on it because he just had dealt with the same questions not long ago. He then honestly informed the emperor

晏殊词作《浣溪沙》意境画

晏殊所作的词《浣溪沙》历来被人们传颂，其中“无可奈何花落去，似曾相识燕归来”成为千古名句。

Artistic Painting of Yan Shu's Poem *Silk-washing Stream*

Yan Shu's poem *Silk-washing Stream* has been widely read. Among the verses, "Flowers fall off unavoidably. Swallows return as before" is well known through the ages.

在书房里读书。皇帝非常赞许地说："闲暇的时候，其他大臣都在外面游玩、应酬，唯有你在读书，真是太子老师的最好人选。"不料晏殊却诚实地回答，其实他本打算出门游玩的，只是因为家里有事，所以才没有出去。皇帝听后，更觉得晏殊为人诚实，当即决定选他做太子的老师。

and requested to change the examination paper. Considering that Yan Shu was very honest, the emperor bestowed on him the title of *Tong Jinshi Chushen* (same as graduates ranked in the third class in the palace examination). Later, the emperor wanted to assign Yan Shu as the prince's teacher, so he came to visit Yan Shu, who was reading in his study. The emperor praised that "in leisurc time, while other ministers either go out to play or engage in social activities, you are the only one who is still reading. You are really the best candidate for teaching the prince." Unexpectedly, Yan Shu honestly replied that actually he also planned to go out but was stuck at home by some domestic matters. After hearing this, the emperor was convinced that Yan Shu was a man of integrity, so he chose him as the prince's teacher right away.

> 守信

中国有句名言："言必信，行必果。"意思是一旦承诺了就必须做到。守信是中华民族非常重视的传统美德。古语有云："人无信而不立。"意思是一个人唯有守信用，才能得到别人的信任和尊重，如此才能与别人建立良好的合作关系。一个民族也只有讲信用才能与其他民族和谐相处。中国人向来重视并且努力践行守信这一美德。

曾子（前505—前436年）是春秋末期著名的思想家。有一次，曾子的妻子要到集市上买东西，年幼的孩子吵着要跟去。妻子不愿带孩子去，便随便对孩子说如果乖乖听话就把家里的猪杀了吃。孩子听了非常高兴，马上就不再吵闹了。曾子得知此事后，真的就把猪杀了。

> Trustworthiness

"Be truthful in speech and firm in action" is a well-known saying in China, meaning that one should have credit. Trustworthiness is a traditional virtue that Chinese people lay great importance upon. As the old saying goes, "A man without credit would not establish a firm foothold." It means that only with credit can a man win trust and respect from others and establish good cooperative relationship with others. Only with credit, likewise, can a nation live in harmony with other nations. Chinese people have always attached importance to this virtue and try hard to practice it.

Zengzi (505 B.C.- 436 B.C.) was a famous thinker in the late Spring and Autumn Period. Once, as Zengzi's wife was going to the market for shopping, their young child repeatedly asked for going with her. His wife didn't want

• 曾子像
Portrait of Zengzi

妻子回家后看到本想要用来卖钱的猪被杀了，非常生气。可曾子却严肃地说："即使是孩子，也不能欺骗，父母更要给他作榜样。假如欺骗了孩子，他将来就可能不守信用。"曾子的妻子听后很羞愧，于是赞同了曾子的做法。

商鞅（约前390—前338年）是战国时期著名的政治家，他在秦国推行变法，使得秦国迅速强大起来，并最终实现了全国的统一。商

to take the child so she half-heartedly promise him that if he behaved well and stayed at home, she would kill the pig for dinner. Hearing this, the child was very happy and immediately stopped asking. After knowing this, Zengzi took it seriously and killed the pig. When his wife got back, she was so angry to find that the pig was killed, which she had planned to sell for money. But Zengzi said with seriousness, "You can't cheat him although he is a child. Instead, we parents should set a good example for him. If you cheat him, he may have no credit in the future." After hearing this, she agreed with what Zengzi had done and was very ashamed.

Shang Yang (approx. 390 B.C.-338 B.C.) was a famous statesman during the Warring States Period (475 B.C.-221 B.C.). He carried out political reform in the state of Qin, which quickly made it strong enough to ultimately unify the whole country. At the beginning of his political reform, in order to gain authority and show his determination to reform, Shang Yang ordered to set up a chunk of wood outside the south gate of the capital city of Qin. Then he promised to the public that anyone who could

鞅在变法之初，为了树立威信，让民众认识到他变法的决心，便下令在秦国都城南门外立一根木头，并当众许下诺言——谁能把木头搬到北门，便赏10金。开始的时候人们都不相信，没有人去搬动木头。商鞅于是增加赏金，涨到50金。一个男子抱着试试看的想法把木头扛到了北门，商鞅马上当众赏了他50金。商鞅的这一举动，使秦国百姓认识到他是一个守信用的人。通过这一举措，商鞅所推行的新法也很快就在秦国推广了。

三国时期曹魏政权的建立者曹

• 商鞅像

Portrait of Shang Yang

move the wood to the north gate would be rewarded with 10 units of gold. At first, nobody believed him, so no one tried to move the wood. Then Shang Yang increased his reward to 50 units of gold. A man attempted to have a try and carried the wood to the north gate. Shang Yang then immediately awarded him 50 units of gold in public, which made other people of Qin realized that he was a man of his word. In this way, the new reform carried out by Shang Yang was quickly promoted in Qin.

During the Three Kingdoms Period, Cao Cao(155-220), the founder of the Cao Wei regime, issued the order of cultivating wasteland and growing crops when he first established the regime. He encouraged soldiers as well as civilians to farm and strictly banned soldiers from trampling crops. Anyone who trampled crops in harvest season would be decapitated publicly. Once, Cao Cao passed by a wheat field when leading his troops to go to battle. On his way many birds suddenly flew out of the

商鞅变法后秦国通用的量器
Common Measuring Device of Qin After Shang Yang's Political Reform

操（155—220年）最初建立霸业时曾颁布“屯田令”，鼓励百姓耕种，同时让士兵也大量开垦荒地，并严令士兵不准践踏庄稼，若是秋收时节践踏庄稼则斩首示众。有一

roadside, making Cao Cao's war horse so frightened that it trod on a large section of wheat. Cao Cao got down from the horse, immediately admitting his error to the official who took charge of laws and asking his punishment. The official didn't dare to punish him, explaining that Cao Cao didn't do it on purpose. What's more, how could the commander of the army be beheaded? Hearing this explanation, Cao Cao cut off a tuft of his hair with a sword and threw it on the ground, saying, "I replaced beheading with cutting off my hair for the moment." In ancient China, hair was considered to be very important as it was inherited from parents. Anyone who cut it at will would be deemed as not filial. So it was a significant move for Cao Cao to cut off his hair to set an example. Cao Cao's strict abiding by the laws spread fast, soldiers and civilians

• 《一言九鼎》装饰画（图片提供：微图）
The Decorative Picture of *One Word Is as Heavy as Nine Cauldrons*

次，曹操领兵出征，路过一片麦田，忽然路边飞出许多鸟，令曹操的战马受了惊，踩踏了一大片麦子。曹操下马后，立刻向主管法令的官员领罚。官员不敢，说这是曹

all admired him and Cao Cao's troops became more disciplined. A few years later, Cao Cao defeated other warlords and unified the north.

操的无心之失，况且一军主帅岂能被斩首。曹操听后，便用剑将自己的头发割下一绺扔在地上，说："暂且用割发来代替斩首。"在中国古代，头发由于是从父母那里继承下来的，因此被看得十分重要，如果随意割掉则属不孝。曹操能以身作则，实在难得。曹操严守军令的事很快就传开了，士兵和百姓无不对他敬佩万分，曹军的军纪更加严明。数年后，曹操打败群雄，统一了北方。

• 曹操像
Portrait of Cao Cao

家庭美德

Family Virtues

家庭联系着个人和社会，是个人和社会之间的中枢。自古以来，家庭在中国都处于非常重要的地位，古代选官员的时候，往往要看他的家庭关系，如果此人不孝顺，或跟妻子、兄弟有矛盾，便不会被录用。家庭由父母、夫妇、兄弟、儿女等成员组成。不同的家庭关系，需要不同的处理方式，譬如儿女对父母应该孝敬，父母对儿女应该教养，夫妻之间应该互相尊重，兄弟之间应该和睦相处。

Family, connecting individuals and society, is the knot between them. Since ancient times, family has held a very important place in China. In officials selecting in ancient times, candidates' family relationship would be examined. If the candidates were not filial, or could not get along well with their wives and brothers, they would not be appointed. A family consists of parents, husband and wife, siblings, children and other members. Different family relationships should be dealt with different approaches. For example, children should show filial piety to their parents, while parents should parent their children. Husband and wife should respect each other and brothers should live in concord with each other.

> 孝敬父母

中国极其重视亲子关系，尤其强调孝敬父母。古语有云：“百善孝为先。”意思是孝在中国的善良品质之中居于首位，所以中国人衡量一个人品质如何，往往看这个人是否孝敬父母。古代在选官员的时候孝敬父母是一项重要的考核标准，汉代更是将《孝经》放在至高的地位上。

西汉时期有一个医生叫淳于意。有一次，他给一个富豪的妻子治病，没能治好，病人没过几天就死了。富豪伤痛万分，将淳于意告上官府。当地官员判淳于意肉刑（在脸上刺字或割鼻、砍足），并将他押解到都城长安（今陕西西安）去受刑。淳于意的小女儿缇萦得知此事，请求要跟父亲同去长

> Filial Piety

China has always attached great importance to the relationship between parents and children, with particular emphasis on filial piety. As the old saying goes, "Filial piety is the most important of all the virtues." It means that filial piety ranks first in Chinese virtues. In this sense, whether a person has good character or not can be seen from whether he is filial to his parents. In selecting officials in ancient times, filial piety was also an important criterion. In the Han Dynasty (206 B.C.-220 A.D.), *Book of Filial Piety* held supreme place.

In the Western Han Dynasty (206 B.C.-25 A.D.), there was a doctor named Chunyu Yi. Once, he treated a rich man's wife who didn't recover and died a few days later. The rich man was so grief-stricken that he took Chunyu Yi to the government office. Chunyu Yi then was

《孝经》

《孝经》是中国古代儒家的伦理学著作，相传为孔子所著。《孝经》较为详细地规定了人应该如何对父母尽孝，主要从物质和精神两个方面着手。物质方面应尽量让父母住得好一些，吃得好一些，穿得好一些等；精神层面应尽量让父母精神愉快，不要让父母再为自己操心。

Book of Filial Piety

Book of Filial Piety was an ethics work of Confucianism in ancient China, which was thought to be written by Confucius. From the perspectives of material and spirit, *Book of Filial Piety* provides detailed rules on how to treat parents with filial piety. From the perspective of material, people should try their best to make their parents live a better life, eat better and wear better. From the perspective of spirit, people should keep their parents happy, not to let their parents worry about them.

- 《孝经》碑帖
  Stone Rubbing of *Book of Filial Piety*

安。来到长安后，缇萦四处求人，将早已写好的奏章交给皇帝。奏章上写道："我的父亲一心救人，如今却获罪受刑。我不但为父亲难过，也为同样受肉刑的人痛心。一个人被砍去了双脚就会成为残废，割去了鼻子便再也不能闻到气味，即使想要改过自新也无法恢复健康了。我情愿为奴为婢，替父亲赎罪。"皇帝看过奏章后，感动于这个女孩儿的救父之心，也很赞同她说的话，于是便废除了肉刑。

汉文帝刘恒（前202—前157年）不仅是谦逊克己的明君，也是

sentenced to corporal punishment (to tattoo in the face or to cut off the nose or the feet) and be escorted to the capital city of Chang'an (now Xi'an, Shaanxi Province) where he would be put to torture. Knowing this, Chunyu Yi's little daughter Ti Ying requested to accompany his father to Chang'an. After arriving in Chang'an, Ti Ying went around seeking for help, and handed the memorial she had written to the emperor. The memorial read, "My father treats people heart and soul, but now he is convicted and sentenced to corporal punishment. I am not only sad for my father, but also for those who are sentenced to this punishment. Without feet one will become disabled and without nose one can never smell. Even if he wants to correct his fault and make a new start, he is unable to recover from the punishment. So I am willing to be a girl slave to expiate my father's sin." After reading the memorial, the emperor was moved by the girl's will to rescue her father, and also quite agreed with what she had said, so he abolished corporal punishment.

• 刘恒亲尝汤药
Liu Heng Tasting Decoction in Person

《二十四孝图》

《二十四孝图》由历代二十四个孝子的故事集成。

The Picture-book of Twenty-four Stories of Filial Piety

It consists of the stories of twenty-four filial children.

- **扼虎救父**

14岁的女孩杨香徒手搏虎，从虎口中救出了自己的父亲。

Clutching the Tiger to Rescue Father

A 14-year-old girl Yang Xiang beat a tiger to rescue her father.

- **拾葚异器**

汉代少年蔡顺年少丧父，又逢饥荒，便拾桑葚充饥，并将红色的桑葚和黑色的桑葚分别装在两个篓子里。黑色的桑葚好吃，供母亲食用；红色的桑葚味道不好，留给自己吃。

Collecting Mulberries in Different Baskets

A boy named Cai Shun in the Han Dynasty (206 B.C.-220 A.D.) lost his father when he was young. During the famine, he picked up mulberries to relieve hunger. He put the red mulberries and black mulberries respectively into two different baskets, because black mulberries were for his mother since they were delicious and red mulberries were left for himself as they tasted bad.

- **怀橘遗亲**

三国时期吴国的科学家陆绩六岁时随父亲拜访朋友袁术。袁术拿出橘子招待，陆绩不吃，而是往怀里藏了两个，拿回去给母亲尝尝。

Hiding Oranges for Mother

Lu Ji, a scientist of the state of Wu during the Three Kingdoms Period (220-280), visited his father's friend Yuan Shu at the age of six with his father. Yuan Shu entertained them with oranges, but Lu Ji did not eat them. Instead, he hid two oranges in his clothes, leaving them for his mother.

- **卧冰求鲤**

晋代少年王祥早年丧母，继母对他并不慈爱，但他仍对其十分孝顺。一年冬天，继母患病想要吃鱼，但河水已上冻，无法捕鱼。王祥便脱掉衣服卧在冰上，待冰融化后再捕鱼给继母吃。

Melting Ice with Body to Catch Carp

A boy named Wang Xiang in the Jin Dynasty (265-420) lost his mother when he was young. Although his stepmother did not love him, he still showed filial piety towards her. One winter, his stepmother was ill and wanted to eat fish, but it was unable to catch fish because the river was frozen. Wang Xiang, however, took off his clothes lying on the ice, and caught fish for his stepmother after the ice melted.

- **扇枕温衾**

东汉少年黄香极其孝敬父亲。夏天，他用扇子将席子扇凉再让父亲睡；冬天，他先用身体暖热被窝再让父亲睡。

To Fan the Mat and Warm the Quilt

A boy named Huang Xiang in the Eastern Han Dynasty (25-220) showed deep filial respect for his father. In summer he cooled the mat with a fan before his father went to bed while in winter he warmed the quilt with his body before his father sleep in it.

- **涤亲溺器**

宋代著名词人黄庭坚自幼侍奉父母。由于母亲不喜马桶的异味，所以他从小就每天为母亲清洗马桶，后来身居高位仍不改变。

Washing Stool for Mother

The famous poet Huang Tingjian of the Song Dynasty (960-1279) attended upon his parents since childhood. As his mother did not like the smell of the stool, he washed it for his mother every day since childhood and continued to do so even after he became a high official.

• 北京密云桃园仙谷岩壁上的雕刻（图片提供：微图）
The Rock Carving in Beijing Miyun Taoyuan Wonder Valley

一个大孝子。他的母亲病了三年，终日卧床不起。刘恒就日夜守护在母亲的床前，照顾母亲的饮食起居。刘恒每次要等到母亲睡着了，他才趴在母亲床边睡一会儿。一旦发现母亲醒来，他便赶紧起身侍奉。刘恒还亲自为母亲煎药，每次煎完，自己总要先尝一尝，看看汤药烫不烫，火候如何，直到自己觉得煎好了，才端过去给母亲喝。刘恒孝顺母亲的事，在汉代流传很

Liu Heng (202 B.C.-157 B.C.) Wen Emperor of the Han Dynasty (206B.C.-220A.D.) was not only humble and self-controlled, but also very filial. His mother had been ill for three years and was bedridden. During the three years, Liu Heng kept a constant vigil by her mother's bedside day and night. He would not even have a nap until he was sure that his mother had fallen asleep. Whenever he noticed that his mother had waked up, he would quickly wake up to take care of

广，朝野上下都敬重他“至孝”。

花木兰（412—502年）是北魏时期的巾帼英雄，因替父从军的事迹闻名天下。花木兰自幼便跟着父亲学习骑马射箭，习得一身武艺。有一年，朝廷大量征兵，她的父亲也在征兵范围内。但此时，父亲已年老多病，木兰不忍父亲受苦，便女扮男装，替父出征。在军营中，木兰跟其他士兵一样风餐露宿，驰骋沙场十余年，屡立奇功，却从未

• 戏剧版画《花木兰》
Opera Woodcut: *A Girl Named Mulan*

her. Liu Heng also decocted medicinal herbs for his mother. Every time he finished decocting, he always had a taste in person to see whether it was too hot, or whether it was well decocted. Only if he thought it was decocted properly, he took it to his mother. Liu Heng's filial piety then was well known in the Han Dynasty, so government officials and the people all admired him as the most filial person.

Hua Mulan was a heroine of the Northern Wei Dynasty (386-581), who was famous for joining army in place of her father. She learned riding horse and archery from her father since childhood, and was versed in martial arts. One year, the government launched a large scale of conscription, and her father was enlisted. But at that moment, her father was old and constantly got sick. Not wanting her father to suffer from hardship, Hua Mulan disguised herself as a man, and went to battle in place of her father. Braving the hardship like other soldiers in the military camp, she served in the army for more than ten years and made her name without being found out that she was female. After the war, the emperor intended to reward her by letting her keep on working for the government, but she declined. Instead, she requested

五伦

五伦是中国古人总结出的五种基本的人伦关系，出自《孟子》，即君臣、父子、兄弟、夫妇和朋友，其中家庭关系占了三伦。孟子认为，君臣之间应有礼义之道，父子之间应有骨肉之亲，夫妻之间应有亲密之爱，兄弟之间应有尊卑之序，朋友之间应有诚信之德，这是处理人与人之间关系的基本道德和行为准则。

The Five Cardinal Relationships

The five cardinal relationships from *Mencius* were five basic human relationships in ancient China, namely, the relationships between rulers and their subjects, between parents and children, between siblings, between husbands and wives and between friends. Three of them deal with the family relationships. Mencius held that there should be propriety and righteousness between the rulers and his subjects; there should be love between parents and children; there should be affection between husbands and wives; there should be order between brothers; and there should be credibility and integrity between friends. These were the basic ethics and codes in dealing with human relationships.

• 孟子像
Portrait of Mencius

被人发现她是女子。战争结束后，皇帝想要奖赏木兰，让她继续为朝廷效力，但木兰谢绝了，她请求皇帝让自己回家侍奉父母以尽孝心。

the emperor to let her return home to take care of her parents with filial piety.

> 教养儿女

孝敬父母和教养儿女是一体之两面，中国人既强调孝敬父母，也强调教养儿女，将孝敬父母和教养儿女放在同等重要的位置上。中国的国学启蒙读物《三字经》中有言“子不教，父之过”，就是说如果子女缺乏教养，这是父母的过错。

孟子是中国著名的政治家、思想家和教育家，在他很小的时候父亲就去世了，母亲一个人带着他生活。孟母非常重视对孟子的教育，为了给孟子营造一个良好的居住和学习环境，曾经带着他搬过三次家。最初，孟子家离墓地很近，很多人前来埋葬死去的亲人，孟子不自觉地学了些丧葬习俗，还经常学死者家属痛哭。母亲觉得这个地方不适合孩子居住，于是搬离了此

> Parenting Children

Showing filial piety towards parents and parenting children are the two sides of one same coin. Chinese people emphasize both filial piety and parenting children and place them in equally important positions. In *Three Character Classic*, an enlightening reading material of Chinese culture, there is a saying, "It is fathers' fault not to parent children", meaning that if children are uneducated, their parents should take the blame.

Mencius was a famous politician, thinker and educator in China. When he was very young his father died and he lived with his mother. Mencius's mother, who attached great importance to his education, moved their house three times in order to create a good living and learning environment for Mencius. At first, their house was near

《孟母断机教子图》（清 康涛）

孟子小时候不喜欢读书，孟母有一天就用剪刀把织好的布剪断，对他说："你荒废学业，正如我剪断织布。布剪断了，就无法接上再织。你错过了学习时间，就会成为一个没有用的人。"孟子听后，从此便开始勤奋读书。

Picture of Mencius's Mother Cutting the Thread on the Loom to Admonish Mencius, by Kang Tao (Qing Dynasty, 1616-1911)

Mencius did not like studying when he was young, so one day his mother cut the woven cloth with scissors, and said to him, "You abandon your studies just as I cut the cloth. If it's cut, it can't be reconnected. So if you miss the time of study, you'll be useless." After hearing this, Mencius began to study diligently.

地。孟子的第二个居所离杀猪宰羊的地方很近，于是他用泥巴捏了很多泥猪、泥牛之类，并用竹片学着屠宰。母亲觉得这个地方还是不适合孩子居住，于是决定将家搬到学

a cemetery, where lots of people came to bury their dead relatives. Mencius then unconsciously learned some funeral customs, and often imitated the bereaved to cry bitterly. His mother thought this place was not suitable for children to live in so they moved away from there. Mencius's second house was near a place for butchering pigs and sheep. So Mencius made many pigs, cows and other animal figurines with mud, and imitated slaughtering with bamboo slices. His mother again thought this place was not suitable for children to live in either, and then she decided to move to a place near school and decided to settle down there,

宫（学校）旁边。这里每个月都举行一些礼仪活动，孟子看到了也跟着模仿，学会了很多礼仪。于是，孟母决定在这里定居。

欧阳修（1007—1072年）是北宋著名的政治家和文学家。他4岁那年，父亲就去世了，家里生活非常困难。母亲郑氏知书达理，非常重视对欧阳修的教育。由于付不起学费，郑氏决定自己教儿子读书。她买不起纸、笔、墨，就拿荻草秆在地上写字，代替纸笔，教儿子认字。经过母亲悉心的教育，欧阳修自学了许多书籍，最终考中了进士。

where Mencius would imitate and learn a lot of etiquette because some ceremonies were held there every month.

Ouyang Xiu (1007-1072) was a famous statesman and writer in the Northern Song Dynasty (960-1127). When he was four his father died, which made life very hard for the family. Nevertheless, his mother, who surnamed Zhen and was educated and reasonable, attached great importance to Ouyang Xiu's education. Being unable to afford the tuition, she decided to teach Ouyang Xiu herself. As she couldn't afford paper, writing brushes and ink sticks, she instead took reed stalks to write on the ground and taught Ouyang Xiu to read. Benefited from her parenting, Ouyang Xiu read many books, and finally passed the palace examination to become a *Jinshi* (a graduate of the palace examination, administered in the capital immediately after the metropolitan examination every three years).

• 欧阳修像
Portrait of Ouyang Xiu

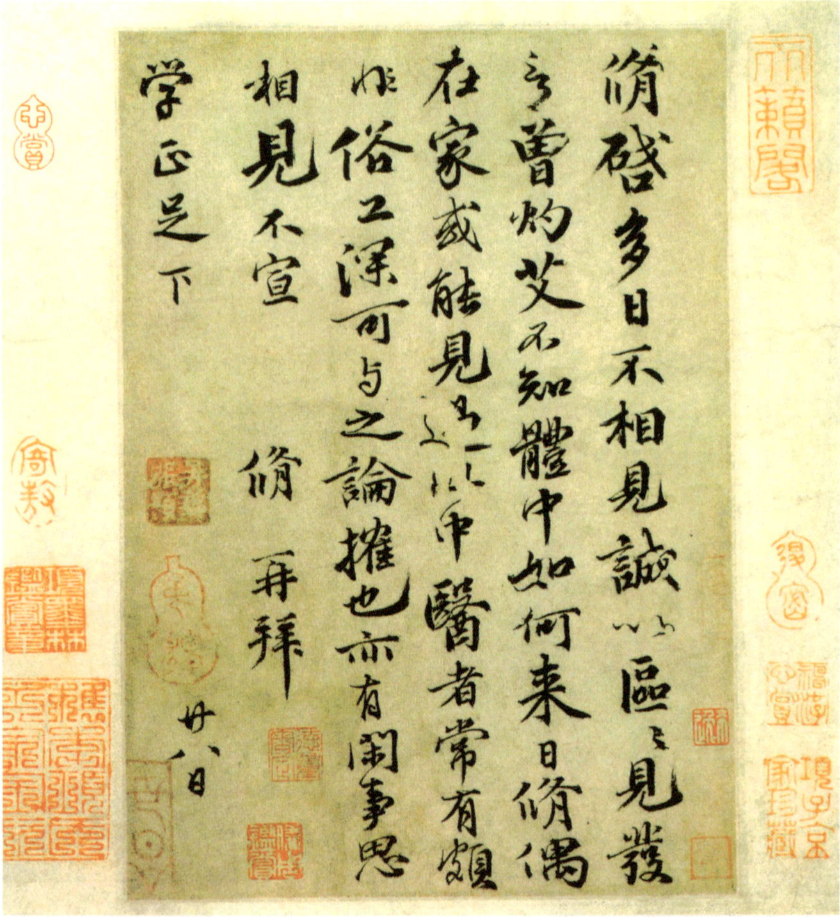

• 欧阳修的书法作品《灼艾帖》
Ouyang Xiu's Calligraphy Work *Burning Wormwood*

寇准（961—1023年）是北宋的名臣，为宋代的国防、政治等方面作出了很大的贡献。寇准小时候家境贫寒，母亲为了供其读书，常常织布到深夜。后来，寇准考中

Kou Zhun (961-1023) was a famous official in the Northern Song Dynasty (960-1127) who had made great contribution to such fields as national defense and politics. He was born in a

了进士，赶紧回家向母亲报告，不料母亲却已病重，去世前写了一封信给寇准，让他在得意的时候再打开看。后来寇准寿辰，大宴宾客，这时他忽然记起母亲的信，于是打开来看：这是一幅画，画着他母亲深夜织布的场景，边上还题着一首诗，诗的大意是希望他能够好好为官，为国家效劳，为民服务，注意自己的品行。寇准看到这幅画和这首诗，不觉流下了眼泪，赶紧撤掉了豪华的宴席。从此，寇准时时以母亲的临终教导提醒自己，终于成为一代名相。

poor family. In order to make money for his education, his mother often wove till late at night. Later, when he passed the palace examination and became a *Jinshi*, he hurried home to inform his mother, only to find that his mother was seriously ill. Before she died his mother wrote a letter to him, which he was to read when he was in his element. Later, on Kou Zhun's birthday, a banquet was held. Then he suddenly remembered his mother's letter so he read it. In the letter there was a picture of his mother weaving late at night, and a poem written on the margin. The poem delivered his mother's expectation that he should serve the country and the people as a good official. Besides, he should maintain good conduct. After watching the picture and reading the poem, Kou Zhun shed tears unconsciously and quickly ended the luxurious banquet. Since then, Kou Zhun always reminded himself of his mother's admonishment and finally became a famous prime minister.

• 寇准像

Portrait of Kou Zhun

> 夫妻和谐

中国古代非常重视夫妻关系，有的经书甚至将夫妻关系列为家庭关系中最为重要的关系，认为丈夫应该尊重妻子，妻子应该理解丈夫。春秋时期的政治家、军事家管子曰："分敬而无妒，则夫妇和勉矣。"意思是夫妇之间应该互相尊敬，妻子不要嫉妒，且夫妻可互为老师，时常指点出对方的错误，以利于个人品德的修养。中国人常用"琴瑟和谐"来形容夫妻关系。琴与瑟是中国的两种传统乐器，它们在一起合奏的时候，所产生的声音非常和谐，因此被用来比喻夫妻关系。

中国有一句谚语："糟糠之妻不下堂。"意思是功成名就之时不能遗弃贫穷时共患难的妻子。晏子

> Affectionate Couple

Chinese attached great importance to the relationship between husbands and wives in ancient times. Some classics even ranked it as the most important one in family relationships, holding that the husband should respect his wife while the wife should understand her husband. The politician and militarist Guanzi in the Spring and Autumn Period (770 B.C.-476 B.C.) once said that husbands and wives should respect each other. She and her husband would teach each other, and often pointed out each other's mistakes to facilitate their moral self-cultivation. In China, the term Harmony of Qin and Se (marital harmony) is often used to describe the relationship between husbands and wives. Qin and Se, two traditional Chinese musical instruments, were likened to the relationship between husbands and wives because

古代夫妻的娱乐活动——下棋
Ancient Couple's Entertainment—Playing Chess

（？一前500年）是春秋后期齐国的政治家、外交家。有一次，齐王欲将爱女嫁给晏子，对他说："你的夫人又老又丑，与你现在的身份并不相配。寡人有个年轻漂亮的公主，让她给你当妻室如何？"晏子一听，急忙谢绝道："臣的妻子确实已经年老，也不漂亮，但我们从年轻时就开始一同生活。当初，她也是既年轻又漂亮的，只是经过了数十载，才从年轻娇美变成年老丑陋。因此，臣绝不能因此而丢弃她。"

古代有一位贤者叫乐羊子，他妻子的品德非常高尚。有一次，乐

their concert can produce very harmonious sound.

There is a Chinese proverb, "A wife who shares her husband's difficulties must never be cast aside." It means when one achieves success and wins recognition, he should never abandon his wife who have gone through storm together with him. Yanzi (? - 500B.C.) was a statesman and diplomat of the state of Qi during the Spring and Autumn Period (770 B.C.-476 B.C.). Once, the king intended to marry his daughter to Yanzi, so he said, "Your wife being old is not a fit match for you considering your status. I have a young and beautiful princess. How about let her be your wife?" Hearing this, Yanzi quickly declined, "My wife indeed is old and not beautiful, but we have been living together since we were young. At that time she was also young and beautiful. It is after decades that she aged and became old. Therefore, I can never abandon her for this reason."

羊子在路上捡到了一块金饼，兴冲冲地拿回家，交给了妻子。可妻子却说："古代品德高尚的人不会要不义之财。丢失金饼的人肯定很着急，你应该把金饼归还给他。"乐羊子听后感到十分惭愧，就在捡到金饼的地方等候了很久，终于把金饼还给了失主。不久，乐羊子出门求学，一年后因思念妻子，提前回到家中。妻子走到织机面前，用刀将织布砍断并说道："我在家里织布，布匹织得很长，但这是一丝一丝积累起来的。这正如你求学，应该慢慢积累，不能半途而废。"乐羊子听后很羞愧，于是再次辞别妻子出门求学去了。在妻子的监督和鼓励之下，乐羊子终于学有所成，成为非常有学识的人。

汉代有一位名士叫梁鸿，许多有钱有势的人都希望能把女儿嫁给他，但梁鸿一直不娶，直到听说有一位虽然长相丑陋但品德高尚的女子孟光，才决定娶她。两人结婚之后非常恩爱，互相尊敬。妻子每次

In ancient times, there was a sage called Yue Yangzi who had a noble wife. Once, he picked up a piece of gold on the road, taking it home excitedly and handing it over to his wife. But his wife said, "In ancient times, a man of great virtues never accept what he doesn't deserve. So you should return the gold to the owner. He must be very worried." Hearing these words, Yue Yangzi was very ashamed, so he waited at the place where the gold was picked up for a long time and finally returned it to its owner. Later, Yue Yangzi went out to study. A year later, he missed his wife so much

• 梁鸿像
Portrait of Liang Hong

• 戏剧版画《举案齐眉》
Opera Woodcut: *Lifting a Tray as High as the Eyebrows*

做好饭端上来的时候，总是把盘子举得跟眉毛一般高，以表示对丈夫的敬重，梁鸿也总是彬彬有礼地用双手接过盘子。所以中国后来就有了“举案齐眉”的成语，意思是夫妻之间应该互相尊重。

张敞是西汉的著名官员，政绩十分卓著，但他在历史上最为著名的事件却是为妻子画眉。张敞和妻

that he came back home ahead of time. His wife then went to her loom and cut the cloth with a knife, saying, "At home I weave the long cloth bit by bit. This is just like your study, in which knowledge should be accumulated bit by bit and cannot give up halfway." Again, Yue Yangzi was ashamed, so he bided farewell to his wife and resumed study. Under the supervision and encouragement of his wife, he finally completed his study and became a very learned man.

In the Han Dynasty (206 B.C.-220 A.D.), there was a distinct personage named Liang Hong, to whom many rich and powerful people were ready to marry their daughters. But Liang Hong never married until he heard that there was a virtuous lady Meng Guang, so he married her. They led a loving marriage and respected each other very much. Every time his wife served him meal, she lifted the tray up as high as her eyebrows to show her respect for him, and Liang Hong would politely took the tray with two hands. That is the origin of the idiom "lifting a tray as high as the eyebrows", meaning that a couple should respect each other.

Zhang Chang was a famous official in the Western Han Dynasty (206 B.C.-

子非常恩爱，他非常喜欢妻子的眉毛，经常亲手为她画眉。张敞在外面也从不遮掩，时时谈及此事，弄得满朝皆知。后来，他为妻子画眉的事传到了汉宣帝耳中。汉宣帝问张敞是不是确有其事，张敞回答道："闺房之乐，有甚于画眉者。"意思是夫妇在闺房之中，还有比画眉更有意思的事情呢，画眉有何不可？汉宣帝从此便将他们树立成夫妻恩爱的典范，后世更是以此为典，津津乐道。

25 A.D.) with outstanding achievements. But he was most known in history for pencilling eyebrows for his wife, with whom he shared deep affection. He loved his wife's eyebrows so much that he often penciled them for her personally, and never bothered to keep this back. Instead, he often talked up the matter so all fellow officials knew about it. Later Emperor Xuan of Han Dynasty heard of his story and asked Zhang Chang whether it was true. Zhang Chang replied, "In couple's entertainment, nothing is more interesting than pencilling the eyebrows for my wife." Hence the emperor set them as a model couple. Later generations also took them as an example, and always talked about them with great delight.

• **张敞画眉**（图片提供：FOTOE）
Zhang Chang Pencilling the Eyebrows

> 兄弟姐妹和睦

中国有一名古话："兄弟如手足。"意思是兄弟姐妹之间如同手和脚的关系，共同承担着维护、传承、兴旺家族的责任，应该互相帮助，一起努力，彼此成全。兄弟姐妹之间和睦相处，对于一个家庭而言非常重要。孔子曰："孝悌为仁之本。"意思是如果一个家庭能父慈子孝，兄弟姐妹之间互相友爱，那么社会就太平了。

中国古代流传着这样一个故事，告诫兄弟们应该紧密团结。相传一位父亲有好几个儿子，兄弟之间不团结，经常发生矛盾。父亲去世之前把儿子们召集在一起，给他们每个人分发了一根筷子，让他们折断。儿子们很轻松地折断了筷子。父亲又把十几根筷子绑在一

> Brothers and Sisters in Concord

China has an old saying that "brothers are like hands and feet", meaning siblings should live in concord like hands and feet. Siblings in a family take the common responsibility of making the family sustainable and prosperous and passing down the family culture. They should help each other, work together and facilitate each other's career. It is very important for them to live in harmony in a family. Confucius said, "The filial piety and fraternal duty are the foundation of benevolence", meaning that in families, if parents are benign, children filial and siblings loving each other, our society will be in harmony.

In ancient China there was a story which admonished siblings to unite closely. According to legend, a father

• 《采薇图》（宋 李唐）
此画描绘了伯夷、叔齐隐居深山以采薇（野菜）为食的故事。
Picture of Picking Wild Plants, by Li Tang (Song Dynasty, 960-1279)
This picture depicts the story of Boyi and Shuqi living in seclusion in remote mountains to pick edible wild herbs.

起，让每个儿子去折，结果他们用尽了力气也折不断这一大把筷子。于是父亲说："你们要是不团结，就像一根一根的筷子，马上会被折断；但如果你们团结在一起，就没有人能够打败你们。"儿子们这才明白父亲的苦心，于是尽弃前嫌，团结在一起，共同维护家族的利益。

伯夷、叔齐的故事是中国古代兄弟和睦相处的典范。相传伯夷和叔齐都是商末孤竹国国王的儿子。国王喜欢叔齐，有心想让他接班，但并没有说出来。国王在去世之前，还是按照传统的方式把王位传给了大儿子伯夷。可伯夷知道这并不是父亲的本意，就将王位让给弟弟，一个人跑到山上藏了起来，让

had several sons who frequently had conflicts. Before dying, the father gathered them together, passed a chopstick to each of them and let them break it. The chopstick was easily broken. The father then tied together a dozen of chopsticks, and let each son break the bunch. They tried with all their might, but no one succeeded. So the father said, "If you do not unite, each of you will be like a single chopstick, which will be broken easily one after another. But if you unite together, no one can beat you." Hearing this his sons understood his implication. So they put the past behind them and united together, jointly safeguarding the interests of their family.

Boyi and Shuqi's story in ancient China is a model of siblings living in

大家都找不到他。叔齐也不愿当国王，于是也跑到山上藏了起来。百姓只得推选国君的二儿子继承了王位。伯夷、叔齐兄弟在当时的历史条件下，不为王位相争而是相让，实属难能可贵。

中国古代著名的孔融让梨的故事，赞扬的就是兄弟之间互相谦让的品质。孔融（153—208年）是三国时期著名的文学家，他小时候就非常聪明，且品德高尚。孔融4岁的时候，有一次父母买了很多梨回来分给他们兄弟吃。孔融的哥哥们都

concord. Legend has it that Boyi and Shuqi were sons of the king of state Guzhu in the late Shang Dynasty. Before he passed away, the king wanted to pass the throne to Shuqi, but he didn't make it public. Instead, he passed the throne to Boyi according to the trandition. Boyi, however, knew it was not his father's intention, so he hid himself in mountains and let nobody find him. Shuqi, also didn't want to be the king, went to mountains to hide, too. Civilians then had to choose the second son of the king to rule the state. It was truly commendable for Boyi and Shuqi brothers not to contend with each other for the throne at that time in history.

Ancient China had a famous story of Kong Rong giving away big pears to his brothers, which praised the virtue that siblings should be considerate towards each other. Kong Rong (153-208) was a famous man of letters in the Three Kingdoms Period (220-280), who was very clever and had noble nature since childhood. Once at his age of four, Kong Rong's parents bought a lot of pear home

• 孔融让梨（图片提供：微图）
Kong Rong Giving away Big Pears

去挑大的梨，唯有他挑了一个很小的梨。父亲看见后觉得很奇怪，于是问孔融原因。孔融回答："我年龄最小，当然应该挑小的了。"父亲听到这番话，非常欣慰。

中国古代兄弟和睦的典范还有班氏兄弟姐妹。东汉史学家班固（32—92年）的父亲没有完成史籍

• 班固像
Portrait of Ban Gu

for Kong Rong and his brothers. When his brothers all picked big pears, he only chose a very small one. Seeing this, his father felt very strange, so he asked Kong Rong the reason. Kong Rong replied, "I am the youngest, so I should choose the small one." Hearing this, his father was very pleased.

The siblings in Ban's family were also set a model of concord in ancient China. In the Eastern Han Dynasty (25-220), historian Ban Gu's (32-92) father died before he completed the writing of the historical work *The History of the Han Dynasty*. Hence Ban Gu determined to follow his father's footsteps and continue the writing. But at that moment Ban Gu was accused by traitors of falsifying the national history and put in prison. The book he had been writing was also confiscated. After Ban Gu's younger brother Ban Chao learned the news, he rushed towards the capital and submitted a memorial to the emperor to explain the truth. After reading the memorial as well as Ban Gu's historical work personally, the emperor highly appreciated what Ban Gu had written and granted him the right to finish the historical writing. Ban Chao (32-102) meanwhile had been

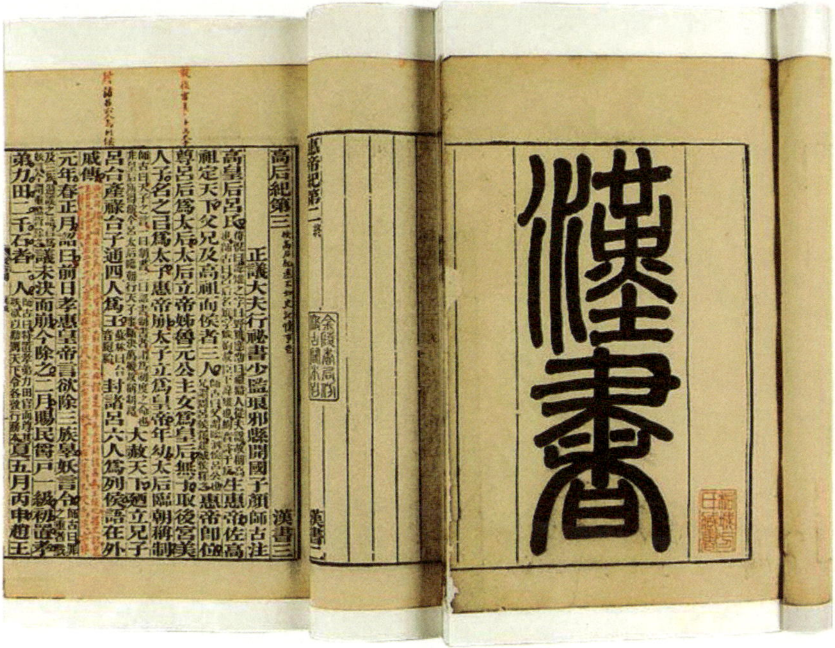

• 《汉书》书影
Photocopy of *The History of the Han Dynasty*

《汉书》的写作就去世了，班固于是继承父志，立志续写《汉书》。但此时班固遭到了奸臣的诬陷，说他私修国史，因此被关进了监狱，所写的书也被没收了。班固的弟弟班超得知这个消息后，昼夜兼程赶到京城，向皇帝上书说明了情况。皇帝看到班超的奏折之后，又亲自

serving in the Western Regions as an officer and diplomat. When he was old, he intended to retire and go back to his home town, but did not get the approval from the emperor. Ban Chao's sister Ban Zhao then petitioned the emperor for her brother, listing Ban Chao's contributions in the Western Regions, and stating clearly her brother's physical condition.

班超像
Portrait of Ban Chao

看了班固的史书，倍加欣赏，于是赐予班固修史的权利。而作为军事家和外交家的班超（32—102年）则出使西域，年老时想告老还乡，可皇帝没有准奏。于是班超的妹妹班昭代兄上书皇帝，列举了哥哥为沟通西域作出的贡献，又说明了哥哥的身体情况，晓之以情、动之以理，希望能够准许他回到家乡。班昭的言语打动了皇帝，终于允许班超告老还乡。

She spoke with reasons and compassion, hoping that her brother could go back home. The emperor was touched by her words, and finally allowed Ban Chao to retire in his old age and to go back home.

社会美德
Social Virtues

中华民族一直非常重视社会美德，因为只有社会关系处理得当，社会才能总体稳定，各种秩序才能正常发展。家庭属于私人领域，社会则属于公共领域。家庭关系因为有亲情在，所以相对简单，而社会关系没有亲情为依托，相对复杂，因此社会美德对于处理好社会关系来说极其重要。一个人在社会中，应该处理好个人与国家的关系，尊重师长、团结朋友、邻里友好、尊重同事，与人为善，这就是我们通常所说的社会美德。

China has always attached great importance to social virtues, because only when social relationship is properly handled, the overall stability of society can be achieved and all kinds of orders can be normally developed. Family belongs to the private realm, while the society belongs to the public domain. Family relationship is relatively simple because it is grounded in kinship, while social relationship is relatively complex because it consists of no kinship. As a result, social virtues are extremely important for dealing with social relationship properly. A person in the society should deal with the relationship between individuals and the state properly, respect teachers, unite friends, be friendly to neighbors, esteem colleagues and bear good intention towards others. These are the components of common social virtues.

> 精忠报国

中国古代讲求“君君，臣臣”，意思是君王要有君王的样子，有帝王风范；大臣要有大臣的样子，忠于职守。三国时期的著名政治家诸葛亮曾说“鞠躬尽瘁，死而后已”，可谓道出了精忠报国的精髓。

大禹是远古时代贤明的君主。在他还是大臣的时候，全国范围内暴发了大洪水。大禹被任命为治水的总指挥，为此奔忙了十几年，曾经三次路过家门而不入。就连妻子生孩子时，大禹也没能回家。后来，民间便以“大禹三过家门而不入”来赞许官员一心为公。

屈原（约前340—约前278年）是战国时期著名的政治家和诗人，他创作的浪漫主义抒情长诗《离

> Serving Motherland Loyally

The tenet of Junjun Chenchen was pursued in ancient China, which means that the monarch should strive to be qualified as a monarch and has a monarch's manner, while officials should strive to be qualified as officials and devote themselves to their duties. As was said by Zhuge Liang, the famous statesman during the Three Kingdoms Period (220-280), "Do my best, until my heart stops beating." His words displayed the essence of repaying the country with supreme loyalty.

Dayu was a wise king in the high antiquity. As heavy floods hit the whole country when he still was a minister, he was appointed as the chief officer to control the floods. Therefore, he went about on his duty for more than ten years, during which he passed by his

• 大禹治水

Dayu Controlling Floods

骚》至今仍被传诵。屈原最初很受楚王重用，因而遭到其他官员的嫉妒。这些官员向楚王进谗言，使楚王日益疏远屈原。屈原最终被贬，之后便写下了长诗《离骚》，既表明了自己的心迹，也为了劝诫楚王。但楚王始终不听他的劝告，使楚国在那些奸佞的治理下愈加衰败，终于被秦军攻入了都城。屈原眼见楚国落到如此境地，绝望地跳江自杀，以死殉国。

岳飞（1103—1142年）是南宋的名将，历史上著名的战略家、军事家，曾为大宋立下了汗马功劳。岳飞小的时候就立志要报效祖国，因此勤奋好学，练就了一身好武艺。相传岳飞参军之前，母亲在他的背上刺了 “精忠报国”四个大

house three times but not stepped into it. Even when his wife gave birth to a child, Dayu was not able to go home. Later, people used the phrase "passing by home three times without entering it" to praise officials who had devoted themselves to public interests.

Qu Yuan (approx. 340 B.C.-approx. 278 B.C.) was a famous statesman and poet in the Warring States Period (475 B.C.-221 B.C.), whose romantic poem *Lisao* is still widely read until today. Qu Yuan at first was entrusted by the king of Chu with a very important position, and thus was envied by other officials. These officials defamed Qu Yuan, making the king of Chu gradually estranged from him. Qu Yuan was eventually demoted. Latcr he wrote the poem *Lisao* to show his loyalty and to remonstrate with the

字，以此激励岳飞，希望他能够为国家作出贡献。后来，岳飞成为一代名将，治军严明，所率领的岳家军骁勇善战。

• 杭州岳王庙
Temple of Yue Fei in Hangzhou

king of Chu. But the king didn't listen to his advice, and made the State of Chu decay more and more under the governance of those treacherous officials. Seeing the State of Chu come to such a situation, Qu Yuan jumped into the river to commit suicide with despair, hoping that his death would awaken the king of Chu.

Yue Fei (1103-1142) was a famous general of the Southern Song Dynasty (1127-1279), who had made great contribution as a famous strategist, militarist and patriot. Yue Fei determined to serve his country since he was a child, and he was studious and well versed in martial arts. According to legend, before he joined the army, his mother tattooed on his back the four Chinese characters of 精忠报国 (pronounced as Jingzhong Baoguo, means repaying the country with supreme loyalty), hoping that these characters could encourage Yue Fei to make contribution to his country. Later, Yue Fei became a famous general and was strict in army discipline, making the brave and battle-hardened Yue's Army almost invincible.

> 尊重师长

中国自古强调尊师重道，将老师与天、地、君、亲并称，可见老师在中国的重要性。中国最早的专门论述教育、教学问题的论著《学

> Respecting Teachers

China has emphasized respecting and honoring their teachers since old times. Teachers ranked equally with heaven, the earth, monarchs and parents, which shows the importance of teachers in China. As

• 清末私塾里的老师和学生
Teacher and Students in Old-style Private School in the Late Qing Dynasty

记》中有言："大学之礼，虽诏于天子，无北面，所以尊师也。"意思是教师给君王讲书是不需要行君臣之礼的。古人称老师为"传道授业解惑"者，他们有着丰富的经验，有着广博的知识，既通过讲课向学生传授知识，也通过自己的言行为学生做出榜样。

子贡（前520—前456年）是孔子的学生之一，后来担任比孔子更高的职位 。孔子去世后，很多学

• 子贡像
Portrait of Zigong

was recorded in *About Learning*, China's earliest works about education and teaching issues, teachers weren't subject to the ritual between rulers and subjects while tutoring the emperor. They were called by ancients as those who impart knowledge, display skill and solve doubts .With rich experience and profound learning, they imparted knowledge to students through lectures, and also set a good example for students through their words and deeds.

Zigong (520 B.C.- 456 B.C.) was one of the students of Confucius, who later held a post more important than that of Confucius. After Confucius died, many students were very sad, and held memorial ceremonies for Confucius, but Zigong was the only one who mourned on Confucius's tomb for six years to show his respect. A lot of people suggested Zigong, "Your position is higher than that of Confucius, and you have more profound learning than him. So why bother to mourn on his tomb?" Zigong replied, "People can easily understand my learning because it is plain, while the learning of Confucius was so deep that most people cannot understand. That's why you think my knowledge is greater that Confucius's." Zigong not only

生都非常伤心，纷纷去祭奠孔子，唯独子贡一个人在孔子的墓前守了6年。很多人都劝说子贡：“你的官位比孔子大，学问也比孔子好，何苦要为其守墓？”子贡说：“我的学问浅薄，别人能够轻易地看到；而尊师孔子的学问深厚，一般人看不懂，所以你会以为我的学问大。”子贡不但尊师，还极力维护孔子的形象和地位，可见他对孔子的敬重。

张良（前250—前186年）是汉朝初年的名将，曾帮助刘邦取得天下。张良年轻的时候有一次在桥上游玩，看见一个老翁把鞋子扔到桥下。老翁让张良帮他捡上来，张良便跑到桥下把鞋子捡上来递给老翁。不料老翁又把鞋子扔到桥下，让张良去捡。张良不解，但还是帮老翁捡了上来。老翁看张良是可造之材，便让他五天之后的早上再到此处，有奇书相赠。五天之后，张良一早就到了，可老翁已经在那里了。老翁训斥了张良，让他五天之后的早上再来。又过了五天，张良赶到后发现老翁还是先到了。第三次相约，张良前一天的深夜就到那

respected his teacher, but also tried his best to maintain the image and status of his teacher, from which his deep respect for Confucius can be seen.

Zhang Liang (250 B.C.-186 B.C.) was a famous general of the early Han Dynasty, who assisted Liu Bang to seize the nation. When Zhang Liang was young, one day he played on a bridge and saw an old man dropping his shoes off the bridge. The old man asked Zhang Liang to help pick them up. Zhang Liang then went down the bridge to fetch the shoes for the old man. Unexpectedly, the old man dropped his shoes down the bridge again, and once more let Zhang Liang pick them up. Although Zhang Liang was puzzled, he helped the old man again. Considering Zhang Liang as promising, the old man asked Zhang Liang to meet him there in the morning five days later because he would give a rare book to Zhang Liang as a gift. Five days later, Zhang Liang arrived at the bridge early in the morning, only to find that the old man was already there, who scolded Zhang Liang for being late, and let him come back again in the morning five days later. Another five days passed, Zhang Liang arrived at the bridge and the old man again was already there. They

• **张良拾履**（图片提供：FOTOE）
Zhang Liang Picking up Shoes

里等候。不久，老翁也到了，看见张良已在那里，非常欣慰，于是传授了一本《三略》给他。张良回到家后认真阅读了这本书，学问大增，后来终于帮助刘邦夺得了天下。

宋代大哲学家程颐（1033—1107年）有一个学生叫杨时，此人品学兼优、德才兼备。有一年冬天，杨时去看望老师程颐，正巧程颐在睡午觉。为了不打扰程颐休息，杨时就站在门外等候。等着等

then decided to meet for a third time. This time Zhang Liang waited there late at night a day before. After a while, the old man came, and was glad to see that Zhang Liang was already there. So he gave the *Three Strategies* to Zhang Liang, who went back home and read this book earnestly. Afterwards his knowledge greatly increased, eventually he assisted Liu Bang to establish the Han Dynasty.

The great philosopher Cheng Yi (1033-1107) of the Song Dynasty (960-1279) had a student named Yang Shi,

• 程颐像

Portrait of Cheng Yi

who has a good nature and great learning, and was competent and virtuous. One winter, Yang Shi went to visit his teacher Cheng Yi, who at that moment was having a nap. In order not to disturb Cheng Yi, Yang Shi stood outside the door and waited. While he was waiting, it began to snow, but Yang Shi still stood outside to wait for his teacher to wake up. After Cheng Yi woke up, he found that the thick snow was at the height of Yang Shi's calves, he was touched very much. Later, this story was widely spread to praise the virtue of respecting teachers.

着，天下起雪来，杨时仍站在门外等老师醒来。程颐睡醒后，发现雪已经没过杨时的小腿了，非常感动。这个故事后来也被广泛传诵，用来颂扬尊师的美德。

> 团结朋友

朋友关系在中国的人际关系中有着重要的地位。中国人喜欢将“师友”并称，老师是长辈，是教授自己知识的人；朋友即是有道义之交的同龄人。孔子曰：“君子以文会友，以友辅仁。”意思是真正的君子用思想、道义去结交朋友，再通过交友来帮助自己更加仁德。《孝经》有言：“士有争友，则身不离于令名。”意思是士人身边有敢于直言劝谏的朋友，就能保持好的名声。

中国一般称朋友为“知音”，这缘于一个故事。古代有一个叫俞伯牙的人，非常善于弹琴，琴艺修养极高。伯牙有一个朋友叫钟子期，非常善于听琴。每次伯牙弹琴，子期都能通过琴声了解到他在

> Uniting Friends

Relationship among friends plays an important role in Chinese ethics. Chinese people like to make the roles of teacher and friend comparable, in other words, teachers are the elder who impart knowledge, while friends are peers who share common morality and goals. As was said by Confucius, a true gentleman seek friends of the same thoughts and morality, and then improved his virtues through learning from friends. *Classic of Filial Piety* also reads, "If a commendable person has friends who are not afraid of speaking the uncomfortable truth, he can maintain a good reputation."

In China, bosom friends are called Zhiyin. There is a story about it. In ancient times, there was a man called Yu Boya, who was very good at playing Qin (a seven-stringed zither) and had achieved

• 《伯牙鼓琴图》（元 王振鹏）

Picture of Boya Playing Qin, by Wang Zhenpeng (Yuan Dynasty, 1206-1368)

想什么，想要表达什么。后来子期去世了，伯牙便再也不弹琴了，并且把自己视若珍宝的琴也摔碎了。他悲伤地说：“我的知音去世了，我也没有必要再弹琴了。”从此，中国人便常用“知音”一词，来形容知己朋友。

《世说新语》中记载了一个关于荀巨伯见义勇为帮助朋友的故事。东汉时有一个叫荀巨伯的读书人，到外地去探望朋友，不料正赶上敌人攻打这位朋友居住的郡城。这位朋友当时正身患疾病，无法逃跑，便让荀巨伯赶紧逃离这里。可

great accomplishment in this aspect. Boya had a friend named Zhong Ziqi, who was very good at appreciating the music played by Qin. Every time Boya played the Qin, Ziqi could understand what he was thinking about and what he wanted to express in his music. After Zhong Ziqi died, Boya never played Qin again. What' more, he broke his precious Qin. He said in sorrow, "There is no need to play Qin any more since my Zhiyin passed away." Since then, Chinese people often refer to their bosom friends as Zhiyin.

The ancient book *Shishuo Xinyu* (*New Anecdotes of the Time*) records the story about Xun Jubo bravely saving

• 壁画《桃园三结义》
Mural: *Three Sworn Brothers in Taoyuan*

荀巨伯却坚持不走，要与朋友共患难。敌人的军队很快占领了城池，很奇怪为什么全城百姓都跑光了，他们却还留在这里。荀巨伯大义凛然地如实告知，并恳求敌军不要伤害朋友，宁愿以自己的性命来换取朋友的性命。敌军头领听后非常感动，觉得荀巨伯对朋友讲义气，也十分勇敢，便把军队撤走，未杀一人。

小说《三国演义》中描写的“桃园三结义”的故事，在中国家喻户晓。刘备（161—223年）是

his friends. During the Eastern Han Dynasty (25-220), there was a scholar called Xun Jubo who went to visit a friend. Unexpectedly, at that time enemy troops attacked the city where his friend lived in. This friend was suffering from illness and unable to escape, so he let Xun Jubo ed without him, but But Xun Jubo insisted on staying with him and sharing hardship together. Enemy troops quickly occupied the city, but wondered why they two still stayed there when all other people in the city fled. Xun Jubo told them the reason and begged the

三国时期蜀国的君主。他还是平民的时候认识了两个朋友，一个叫关羽，一个叫张飞。三人在志向上有相同之处，互相敬佩彼此的为人，于是在一片桃园中结为异姓兄弟。三人一起经历了诸多困难，关系更加紧密。后来，关羽和张飞帮助刘备建立了蜀国。此后，人们就以“桃园三结义”来表示朋友之间应该患难与共，互相信任。

刘禹锡（772—842年）和白居易（772—846年）都是唐代著名的

troops not to hurt his friend. He would prefer to sacrifice himself in exchange for keeping his friend's life. The leader of the enemy troops was touched by his words. Considering that Xun Jubo was brave and loyal to his friend, he withdrew his troops and did not to kill anyone.

Liu Bei (161-223) was the king of the state of Shu during the Three Kingdoms Period. While he was still a commoner, he made two friends, one of whom was named Guan Yu, and the other was named Zhang Fei. Since they had common ambition and respected each other's conducting, they became sworn brothers in a Taoyuan (a peach garden). They three went through much hardship together, and became more and more intimate. Later, Guan Yu and Zhang Fei finally helped Liu Bei establish the state of Shu. After that, people used the phrase "Three Sworn Brothers in Taoyuan" to show that friends should share weal and woe and trust each other.

Liu Yuxi (772-842) and Bai Juyi (772-846) were all famous poets of the

- 刘禹锡的诗作《赏牡丹》意境画

Artistic Painting of Liu Yuxi's Poem *Appreciating Peony*

诗人。二人彼此欣赏，互相支持，友谊深厚，世人将其并称为“刘白”。有一次，刘禹锡与白居易在扬州相逢，相见甚欢。白居易在酒桌上立刻写了一首诗，赠与刘禹锡，并对刘禹锡刚刚被不幸贬职表示了深深的同情。刘禹锡也立刻回赠了一首诗，表示自己已不在乎荣辱，并表达了对好友的感谢。刘禹锡71岁逝世，白居易便写了《哭刘尚书梦得》二首，诗文充满了对好友的怀念之情。

北宋文学家欧阳修的官职很高，文学造诣也颇深，所以有着极高的威望。他的朋友梅尧臣（1002—1060年）的诗文也很好，但家境贫寒，只是一个地方小官。欧阳修并没有因此而轻视梅尧臣，还为他提供了许多帮助和提携。欧阳修是当时文坛革新的领袖，梅尧臣是其主张的积极拥护者，两人互相唱和，留下了很多好诗。有一年，梅尧臣被委派到外地，欧阳修便为其设宴饯行。梅尧臣写诗相赠，表达了他对欧阳修的感激之情。不久，欧阳修被贬职，梅尧臣又专门寄诗劝慰和鼓励他，还采摘

Tang Dynasty. Since they appreciated and supported each other, and shared profound friendship, they were called an inseparable duo. Once, Liu Yuxi and Bai Juyi were unexpectedly met in Yangzhou. The two delighted friends went to have a drink. While drinking, Bai Juyi wrote a poem to Liu Yuxi as a gift, and expressed deep sympathy to Liu Yuxi's demotion. Liu Yuxi wrote a poem right away in return to thank Bai Juyi and to express that he cared little about glory and disgrace. When Liu Yuxi died at the age of 71, Bai Juyi wrote two poems titled *Crying for Minister Liu Mengde*, which brimmed with the memory of his old friend.

In the Northern Song Dynasty (960-1127), Ouyang Xiu held a senior official post and had great attainments in literature, so he enjoyed high prestige. His friend Mei Yaochen (1002-1060) was also excellent in poetic prose, but he was just a minor local official and his family was very poor. Ouyang Xiu, however, did not diminish Mei Yaochen for these. Instead he offered him a lot of help, guided and supported him. At that time when Ouyang Xiu was the leader of literary reform, Mei Yaochen was one

• 梅尧臣像
Portrait of Mei Yaochen

家中的银杏叶，千里迢迢地寄给欧阳修。欧阳修睹物思人，作诗《梅圣俞寄银杏》表示感谢，其中“鹅毛赠千里，所重以其人”这一句被广为流传。

of his active supporters. They two often wrote and read poems together, leaving the world a treasure of poems. One year when Mei Yaochen was appointed to another post, Ouyang Xiu hosted a banquet for him. Mei Yaochen then wrote Ouyang Xiu a poem as a present to express his gratitude. Soon, when Ouyang Xiu was demoted, Mei Yaochen particularly sent poems to comfort and encourage him. Besides, he once picked ginkgo leaves from his house, and posted them to Ouyang Xiu. Seeing the leaves, Ouyang Xiu thought of Mei Yaochen, so he wrote the poem *Mei Shengyu Sends Gingko Leaves* to express his gratitude, among which two verses have been widely read: the gift itself may be as minor as a goose feather, but sent from afar, it conveys deep friendship.

哭刘尚书梦得（之一）

四海齐名白与刘，百年交分两绸缪。
同贫同病退闲日，一死一生临老头。
杯酒英雄君与操，文章微婉我知丘。
贤豪虽殁精灵在，应共微之地下游。

世人称你我二人为“刘白”，我们的友情终生不渝。

我们都想改变日渐衰败的社会局面，经历了多年的宦海沉浮，却终遭贬谪。如今你我一死一生，不能再相见，我也到了老年。

我们志同道合，你的诗婉而多讽，其微言大义只有我知晓。

听说贤人、英雄死后精神不灭，老友到了阴间，应该会有许多贤人、英雄相伴吧。

One of the Crying for Minister Liu Mengde

People call us two as Liu Bai; our friendship remains unchangeable lifelong.

We both wanted to reform the declining society; after many years of ups and downs in political life, we only ended up with being banished from the court. You passed away and I am still alive. There is no way to meet in this world again. What a tragedy for an old man like me.

We have common ambitions and beliefs. Your poems are graceful and tend to be satirizing; only I can understand the real meaning of your sublime words.

It'said that the spirit of the saints and heroes lives forever. My friend must be companied by them.

> 邻里友好

中国人常说"远亲不如近邻"，因为亲戚虽然有血缘关系，但住得太远，一旦有紧急事情发生，亲戚们帮不上忙，而邻居之间却可以及时帮助。因此，邻里之间应该互相谦让，互相帮助，这样才能营造一个良好的居住环境。孔子曰"里仁为美""德不孤必有邻"，意思是应该选择有德行的人作为自己的邻居，如此可以多向他学习；一个人如果品德高尚，就一定会有好的邻居。

东汉时期有一位叫司马徽的隐士，与邻里的关系非常好，凡事从不与邻居相争，而是以谦让为主。有一次，邻居家走失了一头猪，四处都找不到，便到司马徽家里寻找。邻居看到司马徽家也养了猪，

> Keeping in with Neighbors

Chinese people often say that a far-off relative is not as helpful as a neighbor nearby, because although relatives share blood ties, they live too far to help. Once emergency arise, neighbors can offer help in time when relatives' help couldn't reach us. Therefore, neighborhoods should keep in with and help each other, so as to create a good living environment. As was said by Confucius, we should choose a man of virtues as neighbor, so that we could learn more from him. And a person of noble virtues would be surrounded by good neighbors.

There was a hermit named Sima Hui in the Eastern Han Dynasty (25-220) who kept in with his neighbors. He never contended with his neighbors for anything, instead was courteous to them. Once, his neighbor lost a pig and could not find it anywhere, so he looked for it

司马徽像（图片提供：FOTOE）
Portrait of Sima Hui

就认为是自己的那头。司马徽也不争辩，任其牵走了。过了几天，邻居家的猪自己跑回来了。邻居非常羞愧，于是前来道歉，而司马徽却不以为意。

清代有一位叫张英（1637—1708年）的官员，在朝中身居要职，极具威望。有一天，他的家人派人送来一封信，信中说邻居家建围墙多占了他家的三尺地。他的家人前去交涉，邻居却非常不讲道理，于是给张英写了一封信，想让他通过权力找地方官员惩治一下邻

in Sima Hui's house. Seeing that there was indeed a pig in Sima Hui's house, the neighbor was convinced that it was his, so he took it home. Without arguing, Sima Hui just let the neighbor take his pig. A few days later, the neighbor's pig ran back itself. Being very ashamed, the neighbor came to apologize, but Sima Hui did not mind it at all.

There was a prestigious official named Zhang Ying (1637-1708) in the Qing Dynasty, who held a high position at the court. One day, his family sent him a letter, informing him that their neighbor built a fence and occupied three Chi (a length unit in China, equal to about 33.33cm) of their land. His family went to negotiate, only to find that the neighbor was very unreasonable. Hence he wrote the letter to Zhang Ying in an attempt to let him utilize his power to punish the neighbor by the hand of local officials. After Zhang Ying received the letter, he immediately replied. In his letter there was a poem, "Sending me a letter from a thousand Li (a length unit in China, equal to 0.5 km) away only for a wall; why not just give away three Chi to the neighbor.

居。张英收到信后，立即回了一封信，信中写了一首诗："千里修书只为墙，让他三尺又何妨。长城万里今犹在，不见当年秦始皇。"这首诗劝诫家人要息事宁人，让邻居多占三尺又有什么关系呢，不要闹得邻里不和。后来邻居听说了信中的内容，很是羞愧，主动承认了错误，并将新建的围墙又向后退了三尺。这样一来，两家之间空出了一条巷子，有六尺宽，村民们可以自由通过，十分便利，人们便称其为"六尺巷"。

The Great Wall of ten thousand Li is still there today, but its founder the first emperor of Qin can be seen no more." This poem was to persuade his family just to give away three Chi of land to the neighbor, to avoid friction and to keep in with him. Later the neighbor heard of the letter and was very ashamed. He admitted his mistake and made a newly-built fence receding another three Chi. In this way, there was a alleyway between the two families which was as wide as six *Chi*. Villagers could pass through it freely and found it very convenient, as such they called it the Six-Chi Alley.

• 六尺巷（图片提供：微图）
Six-Chi Alley

杨翥是明代身居高位的官员，平日骑驴上朝或外出。他十分喜爱这头驴，每天上朝回家后都会亲自给驴子喂料、喂水。杨翥的邻居是个老翁，快60岁的时候才生了一个儿子，夫妻俩对其非常疼爱。可这个孩子非常害怕驴，一听到杨翥的驴叫就哭个不停，搞得全家人不得安宁。因为杨翥是朝廷中的大官，这家人不敢向杨翥道出苦楚。时间一长，孩子对于驴的害怕与日俱增，饮食也开始减少，身体变得越来越差。当父母的终于鼓起勇气把事情告诉了杨翥。杨翥听说后立刻向邻居道歉，并把驴子卖了，从此外出或上朝都改步行。杨翥身居高位，但并没有因为自己的权势而不尊重邻居的意见，如此也获得了邻居们的尊重。

Yang Zhu was a high-ranking official in the Ming Dynasty (1368-1644), who went to court or elsewhere riding a donkey. He was so fond of his donkey that every day when he went back home he would feed the donkey with fodder and water by himself. Yang Zhu's neighbor was an old man, who finally had a son at the age of almost 60, so he and his wife loved their son very much. The child, however, was very afraid of Yang Zhu's donkey. Whenever he heard the cry of the donkey, he would bawl non-stop, aggravating the whole family. Since Yang Zhu was a senior official in the imperial court, the family did not dare to tell their suffering to him. After a long time, the child's fear of the donkey increased day by day, which made him eat less and less so his health was declining. When the parents finally plucked up their courage to tell Yang Zhu the fact, Yang Zhu immediately apologized to his neighbor, and sold the donkey, afterwards no matter where he went, he was always on foot. Yang Zhu did not ignore the request of his neighbors although he was in high position and had great power, so he won respect from his neighbors.

> 尊重同事

在中国古代，同事被称为“同仁”“同僚”，意思是同事之间应互相促进，同样仁德。而同僚之间又往往互相称为“某某兄”，意思是同事之间应该如同兄弟一样，彼此照应。

管仲（？—前645年）和鲍叔牙是春秋时期两位著名的圣贤之人，年轻时便是朋友，后来成为同事，共同辅佐齐桓公。最初，管仲辅佐的是齐桓公的政敌，后来齐桓公战胜了政敌，鲍叔牙便向他举荐了管仲。而后来，管仲越来越受到重用，并当上了宰相，官职超过了鲍叔牙。但鲍叔牙并不在意，认为管仲的能力本来就比自己强。后来，管仲身患重病，去世前齐桓公问他谁可以继任宰相，鲍叔牙可不可以？管仲回答说鲍叔牙不可以任

> Esteeming Colleagues

In ancient China, colleagues were called fellow workers and workmates, meaning that colleagues should facilitate each other's improvement, and be benevolent and virtuous. Besides, colleagues often called each other brother so-and-so, meaning that colleagues should look after each other like brothers.

Guan Zhong (?-645 B.C.) and Bao Shuya were two sages in the Spring and Autumn Period who were friends since they were young. Later they became colleagues in assisting Duke Huan of Qi. At first, the one Guan Zhong had been assisting was the political opponent of Duke Huan of Qi. When Duke Huan of Qi out-maneuvered the political opponent, Bao Shuya recommended Guan Zhong to him. Later, Duke Huan of Qi trusted Guan Zhong more and more, and appointed him as the prime minister, which was higher than Bao

• 管仲像
Portrait of Guan Zhong

宰相，因为他的性格不适合担此职位，为此齐桓公果然没有任用鲍叔牙为宰相。后来，这些话传到了鲍叔牙的耳中，他非但没有生气，反而很高兴，认为管仲真是了解自己。管仲和鲍叔牙相互了解，知道对方的才干和所能胜任的工作，可谓是真正的知己。

蔺相如是战国时期赵国的宰相，品德与才华都很高。赵国还有一名大将叫廉颇，战功显赫，在赵国的威望也很高。朝中一些小人在廉颇那里挑拨离间说："蔺相如毫无战功，竟然官位比你还高，俸禄比你还多，太不公平了！"廉颇听后，想到自己为赵国立下了汗马功

Shuya's position. But Bao Shuya didn't mind it because he thought Guan Zhong was more competent than him. Later, Guan Zhong was seriously ill. Before he died, Duke Huan of Qi asked him who could succeed him as the prime minister; and whether Bao Shuya was a qualified candidate. Guan Zhong replied that Bao Shuya should not be appointed as the prime minister, because his personality was not fit for the position. So the Duke dropped the thought. Later, Guan Zhong's words were known by Bao Shuya. He was not angry about it, instead he was very happy, because he thought Guan Zhong really understood him. Guan Zhong and Bao Shuya understood each other very well. They really were bosom friends because they knew each other's talents and knew in what position each other could best utilize the talents.

Lin Xiangru was the prime minister of the state of Zhao during the Warring States Period, who had noble virtuous and was enormously talented. The state of Zhao also had a senior general named Lian Po, who enjoyed high prestige in the state because he had made great military achievements. Some devious officials in the court drove a wedge between Lian Po and Lin Xiangru. They said to Lian Po,

劳，但却让蔺相如压在头上，亦觉得心里不平衡。此后，廉颇便处处刁难蔺相如。蔺相如得知此事后，找人向廉颇转达："秦国之所以不敢攻打赵国，就是因为武有廉颇，文有蔺相如。如果赵国的文武大臣失和，内部互相斗争，这不恰恰给秦国以可乘之机吗？"廉颇听后幡然醒悟，便脱掉上衣，背着荆条前往蔺相如家中请求责罚。蔺相如并未惩罚廉颇，反而待之以礼。后来二人互相尊重，和谐相处，共同保卫赵国的安全。这便是成语"负荆请罪"的来历。

"Lin Xiangru has no military achievement, but his position and remuneration are higher than yours. It is so unfair." Hearing this, Lian Po was very indignant because he had made distinguished achievements for the state, but was still dwarfed by Lin Xiangru. Since then, Lian Po always confronted Lin Xiangru. After knowing the fact, Lin Xiangru asked someone to deliver his words to Lian Po. "The reason why the state of Qin dare not attack our state is that we have Lin Xiangru in charge of civil affairs and Lian Po commanding military forces respectively. If we have friction and contend with each other, the state of Qin will seize the opportunity to attack." These words awakened Lian Po. Then he took off his upper coat, carrying thorn twigs on his back and went to Lin Xiangru's home to apologize and to ask for punishment. Lin Xiangru did not punish Lian Po. Instead he treated him with courtesy. Later, they respected and kept in with each other, jointly safeguarding the security of the State of Zhao. Hence the idiom "Carrying thorn twigs to apologize and to ask for punishment".

• 负荆请罪

Carrying Thorn Twigs to Apologize and to Ask for Punishment

> 与人为善

中国古代一直非常强调与人为善的品质。与人为善就是指以善意对待和帮助别人。因为古人深知，世界上大多数人都是陌生人，没有血缘的、道义的、利益的联系，而社会要维持和平与稳定，人与人之间就一定要互相尊敬，和谐相处。在中国古代，陌生人之间也相互称呼“朋友”，就是希望彼此可以成为朋友，或以朋友之礼和朋友之情对待。孔子曰：“君子成人之美。”意思是君子应该尽量成全别人，在别人遇到困难的时候尽可能帮助他。孟子曰：“君子莫大乎与人为善。”孟子认为，君子的品德再没有比与人为善更高尚的了。

相传爱国主义诗人屈原从小就非常善良。有一年，屈原的家乡遭

> Being Kind with Others

Ancient China has always been emphasized the virtue of bearing good intention toward others, which means treating and helping others with good intention. The ancients knew very well that most people in the world were strangers, who shared neither blood relationship nor ties of obligation or benefits. So to maintain peace and stability in society, strangers should respect each other and live together in harmony. In ancient China, strangers also called each other as friend, in a hope that they could become real friends, or could treat each other with friend-like courtesy. As was said by Confucius, "A gentleman is always ready to help others attain their aims", meaning that a gentleman should try to help others to achieve their goals, and help them with his best efforts when they encountered difficulties. Mencius

• 屈原向楚王进策
Qu Yuan Advising the King of Chu

also said, "Nothing is nobler for gentlemen than bearing good intention toward others", meaning that a gentleman would live up to his name when he bore good intention toward others and helped them.

The patriotic poet Qu Yuan was very kind since childhood. One year, famine hit Qu Yuan's hometown, causing many people homeless and begging on the streets. This sad scene grieved Qu Yuan, so he secretly distributed all the rice of his family to the homeless. After his father learned what he had done, he said to Qu Yuan, "Our rice is not limitless. It cannot save so many poor people. If you can be a good official in the future and governed the country well, people will have enough food to eat." Since then, Qu Yuan began to study hard, and finally became an official in a very high position, afterwards he served the country and the people heart and soul, and was deeply loved by them.

饥荒，许多百姓流离失所，沿街乞讨。屈原见此情景非常痛心，便偷偷地将自己家全部的大米拿出来分给百姓。父亲知道后，对他说："咱们家的大米是有限的，救不了这众多的穷人。如果你长大后能做一个好官，将国家治理好，那么百姓们不是都有饭吃了吗？"从此，屈原便开始勤奋读书，终于当上了官员。他为国为民殚精竭虑，深受百姓爱戴。

韩信（？—前196年）是汉朝初年的大将，协助刘邦夺取了天下。

- 韩信像
Portrait of Han Xin

韩信出身低微，年少时家里十分贫穷，只能靠四处蹭饭来维持生活。渐渐地，邻里亲朋都开始厌烦他。于是，韩信离开了家乡，寻找出路。路上，他饥寒交迫，几乎要饿晕了，一个以洗衣服为业的老妇人看见后，就送给韩信一些吃的，如此持续了好多天。韩信非常感激，承诺老妇人有朝一日一定会报答她。后来，韩信成为汉朝建立的重要功臣，亲自酬谢了这个老妇人。

Han Xin (?-196 B.C.) was a senior general of the Han Dynasty, who assisted Liu Bang to seize the country. He was born in a humble family. When he was young, he had to beg around for food. As his neighbors, relatives and friends gradually grew tired of him, Han Xin left his hometown to find a way out. On his way, he was suffered from hunger and cold, and almost faint with hunger. When an old laundrywoman saw it, she provided Han Xin with food, fed him for days. Being grateful, Han Xin promised to repay her some day. Later, he became an important hero in the founding of the Han Dynasty. He then rewarded the old woman personally.

《西游记》中的与人为善

《西游记》是中国古典四大名著之一，讲述了唐僧去印度取经的故事。唐僧师徒四人路上经历了千辛万苦，也得到了许多陌生人的帮助，譬如途中找不到旅店，就只好借宿在陌生人家里。很多老农或乡绅不仅热心地留他们住宿，还供给他们食物和水，这也是他们能够成功取经的关键。同时，《西游记》中也有很多唐僧师徒帮助陌生人的故事。他们住到陌生人家里，若发现主人家中有强盗来袭或被妖怪骚扰，便会帮助他们打退强盗，除掉妖怪。唐僧师徒与陌生人之间互相帮助，互相提供方便，为人与人之间的相处树立了榜样。

Bearing Good Intention Toward Others in *Journey to the West*

Journey to the West is one of the four Chinese classics, telling the story of Tang Monk going on a pilgrimage to India for Buddhist scriptures. Tang Monk and his three disciples suffered innumerable hardships on their journey, but also got a lot of help from strangers. For

• 版画《西游记》
Woodcut: *Journey to the West*

• 唐僧师徒雕像（图片提供：FOTOE）
Statues of Tang Monk and His Disciples

example, when they couldn't find inns on their way, they had to stay overnight in strangers' houses. Many farmers or squires not only accommodated them with hospitality, but also treated them with food and water. This was crucial for them to succeed in obtaining Buddhist scriptures. Meanwhile, *Journey to the West* also consists of a lot of stories about Tang Monk and his disciples helping strangers. Whenever they lodged in strangers' houses, if they discovered that the host families were robbed or attacked by monsters, they would help them defeat robbers and repel monsters. Tang Monk and his disciples and strangers helped each other, and provided each other with convenience, setting a good example of bearing good intention towards strangers.

与自然界相处的美德

Virtues in Interacting with Nature

中国自古就有“天、地、人三才之道”的说法，强调“人法地，地法天”，意思是人有其局限性，不能完全地认识天地，也不能控制自然，因此人在天地和自然面前都应当谦卑。中国人主张对于自然资源的开采应有度，也应顺其自然，与自然和谐相处。

Chinese since ancient times have understood the way among heaven, the earth and man and stressed that man should follow the law of the earth, while the earth follows the law of heaven. It means that man have his limitations. He is unable to fully understand heaven and the earth, and unable to control nature either. So in front of heaven, the earth and nature, man should be humble. Chinese people always advocate moderately exploiting natural resources. Besides, we also agree to let nature take its course, and live in harmony with nature.

> 敬天

中国人从古代起就注重“敬天”，即按照大自然的运行规律行事，而不是盲目地按照人类的私

> Cherishing Nature

China from ancient times to present holds the virtue of cherishing nature, namely, to act in accordance with the laws of nature, not to follow the drive of human

• **北京天坛祈年殿**

天坛是明、清两代帝王祭天和行祈谷礼的地方。

Hall of Prayer for Good Harvest in the Temple of Heaven in Beijing

The Temple of Heaven is where emperors of the Ming Dynasty (1368-1644) and the Qing Dynasty (1616-1911) held ceremonies to worship heaven and pray for good harvest.

• **清代同治皇帝在天坛举行祭天大典**（图片提供：FOTOE）
Emperor Tongzhi of the Qing Dynasty (1616-1911) Held a Ceremony to Worship Heaven in the Temple of Heaven

心行事。古人还提出“天人感应”之说，即如果天有异常现象，人类应该先反省自身，分析是不是由于人类的错误或过失造成了自然的灾难，然后加以改正。中国历代帝王都有祭天的习俗，以此来表达人们对于大自然哺育万物的感恩之情，并祈求上天保佑天下百姓。

selfishness blindly. The ancients also proposed a saying of "empathy between nature and man", meaning that if heaven had abnormal phenomenon, man should first self-examine himself and analyze whether the abnormal phenomenon was caused by man's faults, and then corrected them. Chinese emperors of successive dynasties had the custom of worshipping heaven to express people's gratitude to nature for nurturing all things on earth, and to pray to heaven for blessing people in the world.

• 模仿清代祭天仪式的表演（图片提供：徽图）

Recreation of the Performance of Ceremony to Worship Heaven

> 用之有度

中国自古以来对自然资源的开采和利用都讲究适度，反对对自然资源进行掠夺式开发。在这样的指导思想之下开发利用自然资源，既能满足人的生活需要，也能保持自然资源的循环再生。

孔子曰："钓而不纲，弋不射宿。"意思是钓鱼可以，但不能将鱼一网打尽；射鸟可以，但不要去射归巢歇息的鸟。这就是要求人们向大自然索取要有度，不能过分贪婪。孟子也认为，伐木者应该"以时入山林"，意思是春天万物生长的时候不能随意砍伐。中国古代很多行业都有其行规，譬如捕鱼业要求渔网的网眼不能太小，以免捕到鱼苗，另外在鱼类繁殖的时节也不能捕鱼，否则会遭到同行人的谴

> Exploiting Moderately

Since ancient times, China has been insisting on modest exploitation and utilization of nature and against predatory exploitation. Exploitation under this guiding notion not only can meet people's needs but also observes the cycle of natural resources.

Confucius said that "we can fish, but we cannot catch all the fish at one go; we can shoot birds, but we cannot shoot birds that rest in nests." His words in fact required that people should not be greedy. Instead, we should insist on moderate exploitation. Mencius also held that "spring is the time for many things to grow; loggers should not cut down tree at will." In terms of moderate exploitation, different sectors had different regulations in ancient China. For example, in fishing industry, meshes on fishing nets could

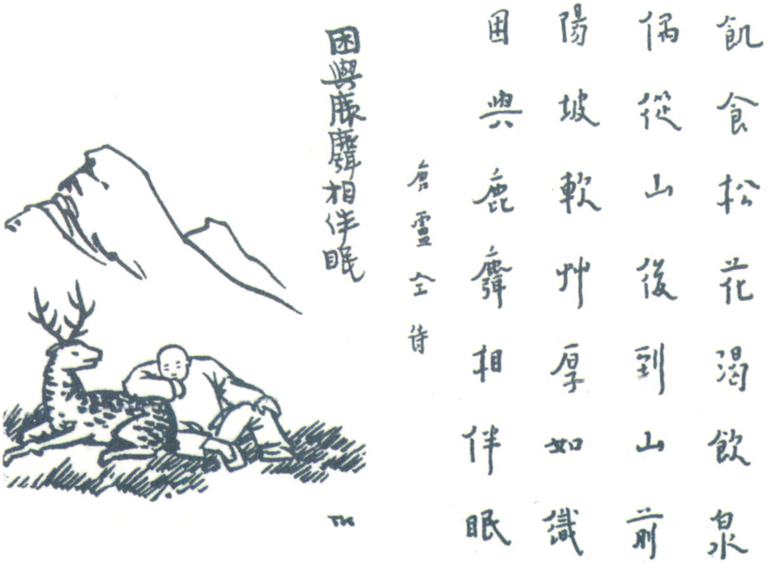

• 《护生画集》（丰子恺）

丰子恺是中国现代著名的文学家和画家，他曾画过一本《护生画集》，目的就是希望人们爱护生物。

Painting Album of Protecting Living Things, by Feng Zikai

Feng Zikai (1898-1975) was a famous writer and painter in modern China. He created the *Painting Album of Protecting Living Things* in a hope that people could protect living things.

责；狩猎业要求不能猎杀小兽，也不能猎杀怀孕的母兽；伐木业要求砍掉几棵树，就要再种上几棵树，不能只砍树而不种树。这些行为的倡导都是为了资源的可持续发展，是用之有度的表现。

传说有一年春天，哲学家程颐陪着皇帝一起出去游玩。皇帝见春

not be too small, so as not to catch fries. Besides, in breeding season, people cannot fish or they would be condemned by fellow fishers. In hunting industry, hunters cannot hunt cubs and pregnant female animals. In logging industry, when people cut down trees, they were required to plant the same amount. Cutting down trees without planting

色很好，兴之所至，折断了一根柳树枝。程颐见状，立即对皇帝说："春天不能折树枝，因为这样会伤害春天的生机。按照大自然运行的规律，春天是万物生长的季节，所以不能轻易去折断柳枝，妨碍树木的生长。如果人人都折断一段树枝，那么就不会再有树木了。"皇帝听后觉得程颐的话很有道理，便下令以后每年春天全民都不允许采摘植物的新枝。

new ones was prohibited. These were examples of moderate exploitation to maintain sustainability of resources.

One spring, philosopher Cheng Yi accompanied the emperor on a sightseeing tour. The emperor was so delightful to see the beautiful spring landscape that he broke off a twig from a willow tree. Seeing this, Cheng Yi immediately said to the emperor, "Never break off a twig in spring. According to the law of nature, spring is the growing season for all things. So never break a twig from a willow tree at will, because it will hinder the growth of the tree. If everyone breaks off a twig, there will be no more trees." Hearing this, the emperor thought Cheng Yi's words were very reasonable, so he ordered that no one was allowed to break off new twigs every spring.

• 春天的树林
Spring Woods